Purchased by me out of
Birthday money from Nan

Nov 1992.

SUPERSTITIONS

SUPERSTITIONS

PETER LORIE

SIMON & SCHUSTER

LONDON·SYDNEY·NEW YORK·TOKYO·SINGAPORE·TORONTO

First published in Great Britain by
Simon and Schuster Ltd in 1992
A Paramount Communications Company

Simon and Schuster Ltd
West Garden Place
Kendal Street London W2 2 AQ
Simon and Schuster of Australia Pty Ltd. Sydney

A CIP Catalogue record of this book is
available from The British Library
ISBN 0-671-71141-5

Superstitions was created by Labyrinth Publishing
Design by Malcolm Godwin
Printed and bound in Germany by Mohndruck GmbH, Gutersloh
Typesetting by The Dorchester Typesetting Group Limited, England.

*The publishers wish to state that there are many herbs and plants that can cause
sickness and can poison the body or cause hallucinogenic effects to users. If there is
any doubt as to the use of any herb or plant either included in this book or not, the
reader is advised strongly to consult a good herbal or speak to a pharmacist,
doctor or homeopathic doctor. The publishers cannot accept any responsibility for
any damage suffered from the use of herbs and plants and remedies included
in this book.*

CONTENTS

Esbat. The Witches Frolic
by George Cruikshank 19th c.

INTRODUCTION

Risks of the Day

HOW MANY TIMES have you gone to work in a bad mood and someone has said "Well, you sure got up on the wrong side of the bed this morning"?

How often have you avoided walking under a ladder, or felt some trepidation at an up-coming Friday the 13th?

These things are so common today that we barely give them a thought. We observe the superstition as part of our normal life.

But how many superstitions do we commonly employ each day? And how many things do we do, habitually, without realizing that they are superstitions that may be based on sources often centuries old?

Before moving deeper into the lore and sources of the hundreds of common and not-so-common superstitions, we might first take a look at a superstitious day and see what the many pitfalls are that could face us.

If your response to this is "I'm not a superstitious person," take a closer look at the next few pages. Read between the lines and let us come again to the same question: how superstitious are we?

You wake up to the sound of your alarm clock and you notice that it's Friday the 13th! You're immediately in trouble. This could be the unluckiest day of the year, so you get out of bed on the wrong side and bump into the wall!

You stagger into the bathroom to look into the mirror and find that it has fallen to the floor and shattered. Seven years of continuous bad luck begins today. Friday the 13th was right. It really is your unlucky day, but it's not over yet.

Food figures prominently in the superstition stakes, but mostly in relation to bad cooking. The devil seems rarely interested in the gourmet kitchen for he prefers to sample failure rather than success. You are now faced with suffering a fate worse than death as you make a breakfast this dangerous morning. In the preparation of the coffee and eggs there are cautions to be observed at every turn. Don't stir your companion's cup as this will stir up strife.

Don't spill the milk for this is the worst luck. Don't then boil over the milk or you add to the problems, and don't open the boiled egg at the small end or you offend the fates even more. If you have managed to break one or all of these rules, then it is essential the following rhyme is chanted:

"Break an egg: break your leg. Break three, woe to thee; break two, your loves true. You may be sure that if I break one, I take good care to break another one as well." With luck, this may bring the balance back to normal.

As you leave the house on your weary way to work, two clocks chime simultaneously. Now, for the first time in the day, this piece of coincidental bad management might not actually cause you any personal hardship. But a poor unfortunate couple somewhere in your town will probably die as a result! But by this time you have become so paranoid that you are watching out for anything that might offend the fates. You look down at your shirt and you realize that you have put it on inside-out. Disaster! You return home quickly and put the shirt on properly. Ah, what a relief, for you have in one rapid act turned your bad fortune to good. You have wiped the slate clean and can start afresh without a care in the world.

But wait, there's a button missing from the shirt. Time is running short and you must rush to get to work on time, so you sew on the button without taking off the shirt. Disaster. You will have bad luck for the rest of the day, and someone will speak ill of you.

Oh well, at least one day's bad luck is better than seven years. Given a full understanding of superstitious ritual you could in fact make a balance sheet of it, the "bottom line" being the worst or best luck you could have under the circumstances. So far, we are not doing badly at all.

1.
Don't stir another's cup for it will stir up strife.

7.
Spilt milk is the worst

2.
Daffodil hangs towards you. Bad omen!

4.
Broken egg: break your leg. Open the (boiled) egg at the small end: You'll come to a bad end.

3.
Shoe on table. A serious quarrel in the home.

5.
Burnt toast feeds the devil.

LIFE & TIMES

FRIDAY MARCH 13 1992

Coping with life,

FRIDAY 13

12.
Friday 13th is unlucky enough
but if you leave the calender
at this date the devil will claim
you on the 14th.

13.
Not only Friday the 13th but
the unlucky mad month of
March as well.

8.
Look in the tea leaves.
Whatever you are thinking of
will come true.

11.
Don't consult the stars on the
13th.

6.
Knife points towards your own death.

10.
Broken mirror. Seven years
bad luck from today!

9.
Spilt salt. Unless you act
quickly the devil will punish
you.

Out into the street again and that same clock strikes simultaneously with the church bells. For sure there will be a fire in the town, a pretty safe bet in modern towns. But to make matters worse, you speak with a friend that passes while the clock is still striking – more bad luck. And all that shirt-changing has given you a chill. You sneeze without putting your hand in front of your mouth. Now you're in real trouble for your soul has unceremoniously escaped from your body. Just your luck. And on a day like today. You haven't even got to the train station yet!

You arrive at the station and get on the train. Amazing really, when you think of your luck so far, that you've managed to survive without falling under the wheels of the train and dying on the spot! But, oh dear! You look down at your shoes and realize that not only have you got a broken shoelace but you have put your shoes on the wrong feet!!

Now, apart from the intense embarrassment involved in sitting on a crowded commuter train and having to switch around your shoes, but also having to display to everyone present that you are walking around like a bum with broken shoelaces, both these events will have added to your barometer of bad luck by several points. In your rising sense of unease you place the offending shoe on the table of the train compartment. Oh my God! For sure there will be a serious quarrel in your household when you get home that night, and thunder and lightning will strike before too long. The shoes must never after be worn if placed on a table, for such shoes can only thence forward be employed for the long walk into the underworld!

So, in the midst of clashing skies, broken shoelaces, sore feet, and impending household unrest, to say nothing of a mountain of bad fortune hanging around your neck like an albatross, you stagger in to work, fall headlong through the door of your office and slump into your desk chair in the certain knowledge that if the day isn't your last then for sure you will be fired from your job, have a serious accident in the traffic, and end up divorced and mutilated for the rest of your life. Better not budge. Stay put for the whole day and perhaps you might avoid the fates and their devastating rigors. Who knows, you might be luckier this afternoon.

But you still have to get through your lunch without event. You decide, given the uncertainties of the morning and the fact that your horoscope in the morning newspaper was not very encouraging, to stay in for lunch. You make some toast in the office kitchen and boil water for a packet of soup you managed to get from your office neighbor. So far, so good. But in your agitated state you manage to burn the toast so badly that it catches fire in the toaster, and as you attempt to save the blackened charcoal from setting the whole office on fire, you turn again to the kettle and pour the boiling water into an empty pot.

Oh dear, once again. Burning bread is about as unlucky an act as you could perform for burned bread, not unnaturally, feeds the devil, while pouring boiling water into an empty pot brings its own brand of misfortune; and we all know that on a

Above: ***Lucifer*** *from the Douce Collection, Bodlean Library, Oxford*
Superstitions are seldom logical. For instance, the devil who lurks behind your shoulder waiting to see you spill salt is hardly likely to be Lucifer himself. Even the most cravenly superstitious would concede that the Great Adversary might have more important and fiendish affairs to attend to than spilt salt. Doubtless then it would be a very minor bureaucrat of Hell who would actually get it in the eye.

Friday the 13th like this Friday the 13th, the devil is lurking very close behind your shoulder preparing to avoid the salt that you will for sure be throwing into his eyes before long.

Eventually, somehow or other, the day ends and you are still miraculously alive and in one piece. Time to take the risk of going home! Outside the office you see a beautiful daffodil, but beware for its head is hanging toward you. On the balance sheet of your fortune, there is one year of bad luck in your favor. You walk under a railroad bridge, muttering to yourself about this terrible Friday the 13th, and you do add to your bad fortune, for talking beneath a bridge is not advised. Looking up at the sky you see a raven fly past, and its squawk sounds as though it has choked! Walking with your head in the air you forget that you are walking on the lines of the sidewalk, and simultaneously you also walk under a ladder and that new shoe lace you put into your shoe comes untied! You may as well give up right now because you have encouraged all the bad luck that exists in the world to fall at your feet. It's over!

It starts to rain (of course!), and as you arrive home you forget to put your umbrella down before entering the house. Your calender shows tomorrow's date, and as you sit down in a chair it falls over. Your spouse will know at once that you have been lying.

As you sit down for your evening meal, you thoughtlessly spin the dinner knife and it points back toward you. Now the end really is nigh for this one gesture points to your death. How much worse can things get?!

And so we meet the devil over dinner. It seems almost as though we can barely avoid him when it comes to feeding time. Water spilt, salt spilt, dropping a fork or a piece of meat. All these things will permit him to lean closer over your shoulder, where he normally waits for these mistakes to occur. Take up the salt from the floor and quickly throw it into his eyes, right to left, over the shoulder, and you may blind him for long enough to escape the moment of bad fortune. Salt is the saving grace, for it is the purest substance on earth and stronger than holy water which you are unlikely to have on tap anyway. Keep a few spare bags of pure salt around the house for emergencies, and give one to your favorite guest as he leaves the house. This will store up your joint good fortune for the future like a savings account of luck, with interest.

Before the day is over, now that you have become ultimately wary of all the signs of bad fortune, there are still many things you must look out for.

Beware of the child bursting a paper bag. Be careful not to stumble on the stairs. Look out for the black cat that crosses your path. Don't let visitors to the house poke the fire or place the fire tongs on the table, and be sure that your dinner guest does not fold the dinner napkin onto the table – in so doing he will have folded up the friendship between you.

And finally as you make your weary and battered way to bed, be sure that the bed has not been moved so that the foot faces the door. To be sure that you sleep without bad fortune for the next day (Saturday the 14th, thank God), fold the pantyhose or stockings of the woman of the house across the foot of the bed with a pen placed inside the folds. With this important arrangement, nightmares of the disastrous day that you have just lived through will not haunt the night.

This extraordinarily hazardous, and fortunately unlikely, day gives us a flavor of how it would be to exist with superstition. Life for the average country dwelling peasant in Medieval Europe would have been filled with every conceivable device for warding off the influences that might be created by such events. The household was filled with herbs, flowers, salts, holly leaves, garlic, and all sorts of items that could be taken up in defense of the incomprehensible, and therefore potentially dangerous fortunes of life. This was hundreds of years ago and had been continuing as a way of life for thousands of years before that. What superstitious people they were! And yet what about today? How many of these stories do we still take seriously, even if our tongues are slightly embedded in our cheeks?

How about getting out of bed the wrong side and breaking a mirror? What about the ladder and the fallen salt, the burnt toast and the spilt milk, the black cat and the passing raven, and sneezing without placing the hand before the face? And what about the lines on the pavement, the spinning knife, and many other seemingly innocent events such as opening an umbrella in the house and kissing under the mistletoe? There are literally hundreds of such common daily activities which we still observe with some trepidation. We may have lost the original meaning and we may cast doubts as to the real dangers involved, but don't most of us prefer to observe the ancient lore, just in case?

WHY SUPERSTITION?

EVERY AGE PAYS ATTENTION to the ancient superstitions according to a certain subtle fashion, very often knowing nothing about the original lore or sources from which they derived. It wasn't so long ago that bibles were fanned in front of sick men's faces and communion wine was prescribed for whooping cough while women bathed their sore eyes with baptismal water. Although modern westerners would not admit to crossing themselves when faced with potential evil such as a passing magpie, they do cross fingers to prevent bad luck. Some superstitions merely transform from the original, and the original is frequently a relic of still more ancient cultures and long-vanished ways of life. Above all, superstitions remain as outward expressions of the tensions and anxieties that hold sway over humanity as it struggles down the corridor of life from birth to death, buffeted by change and uncertainty.

We can see the superstition, therefore, as a constancy; a kind of reassurance against fluctuation as though we are part of an impenetrable mystery with incomprehensible rules.

To Christians the original "pagan" beliefs were superstitions while to the Protestants the use of rosaries was a superstition, and to the Puritans the decorations carefully displayed in any cozy house during Christmas were superstitions, especially the use of ivy or mistletoe or holly.

And yet – strangely perhaps in this age of reason – it very often turns out that we are more interested in the mysteries of superstitions than in previous centuries when they were taken for granted, and that in fact there is much more to many superstitions than is at first obvious. Mistletoe, for example, was the most holy of plants to the Druids, why so? To hang a sprig of this strange plant in a house at Christmas is to attract young men to kiss young women beneath it, each time plucking one of the berries from the sprig. Why should this be so? Who started it? What were the properties of mistletoe that promoted fertility in women? Why did the hanging of mistletoe keep away the devil? The young woman to whom the man had given the plucked berry would retire to her room, lock the door and swallow the berry. She would then inscribe the initials of the man onto a mistletoe leaf and "stitch it into her corset close to her heart, binding him to her so long as it remain there."

Hanging Mistletoe in Victorian England from a Ladies Journal of 1885

Superstitious nonsense! But how do we maintain the best love affairs, the best and most happy relationships? By mutual concern, by bringing the partner close to an open heart, by honesty and warmth, by acknowledging their presence in our lives. How better to represent this than with a mistletoe leaf inscribed and secreted in the most intimate place?

During the years following the seventeenth century, witchcraft was seen as almost an epidemic form of superstition with all manner of terrors available to the ignorant and even the intelligent individual. Couples about to be married would be forced into the most complex rituals in order to untie any witchy influence, including and especially the untying of any knots in their clothes that might contain a witch's spell. There were so many significant objects that could not be accepted as gifts that the intended couple could barely set up their homes without serious danger of witchcraft; pins, shoes and knives were absolutely taboo, and if the man happened to be a fisherman and one of his guests inadvertently borrowed something from his fishing boat there would be hell to pay because the luck of the fishing goes with the article.

But there were always as many white magic remedies available in witchcraft as there were black. It was not always bad fortune that resulted from the presence of magic, and magic played a big part in superstitious belief.

It was believed that the knots in a piece of string or thread could both endanger a birth and cure a strained wrist. A black cat could bring evil or its blood cure disease, the sacred white horse gained good fortune by being spat at, and the black-faced chimneysweep brought good luck if kissed! Evil could always be turned away through the various recognized means, such as casting a pure substance over the shoulder or by turning and facing the source. There was never only one way to go.

All superstition has grown from something, there is no smoke without fire. Who was the first one to decide that opening an umbrella in a house

is bad luck? Who was the first to walk under a ladder and suffer the consequences? Who hung a horseshoe the wrong way up, smashed a mirror, and spilled salt to spend a life-sentence at the hands of the fates? Who first branded Friday the 13th as a day on which luck would run out? What was the world like that produced and maintained such extraordinary ideas?

The bulk of the population, aside perhaps from the aristocratic classes, was concerned largely with the search for or production of food; therefore the changes of the seasons, the success or failure of the crops and all the influences that nature had upon life. The greater part of the populations of Europe lived in rural areas in small isolated communities. The difference between rich and poor was marked, and 99 percent of the people were very poor. Even as late as seventeenth century England around two-thirds of the adult male population were unable to read and would sign their names with an "X".

Life was extremely hazardous, and the central feature of day-to-day existence was a preoccupation with the explanation for and relief of human misfortune. If you lived in a small hovel or the base of a tree, the vagaries of the climate, your very often hostile neighbors or robbers and vagrants that passed by, were of constant concern to you.

In seventeenth-century Europe, for example, life-expectancy was influenced by the constant presence of sickness and premature death. The average life-expectancy at birth of boys born in the last part of that century was just under 30 years. Today it is around 70 years. One-third of the children within the aristocracy died before the age of five.

Food supply, of course, was totally reliant on the success of harvests in the local areas. Each family went either to the local farms and bartered goods for food direct from the land, grew it themselves, or at best went to local village markets. If an epidemic of bubonic plague happened to coincide with a poor harvest, the population could suffer as much as a 50 percent loss in one year! The seventeenth-century plague in England, for example, killed 34 percent of people living in the London area. It is said that the greatest reason why this particular epidemic was stopped was the Great Fire of London in 1666 which literally burned the dirty and rat-infested buildings to the ground and thus ended the spread of disease. Living in these times was like jumping from the frying pan into the fire.

The main causes of disease were readily seen to be derived from supernatural sources, and the only form of psychotherapy was provided by the clergy. Physicians were regarded with the greatest suspicion and "avoided like the plague" they sought unsuccessfully to cure.

Helplessness in the face of disease and suffering was perhaps the most essential element in the background to the beliefs of superstition, but not the only reason. There was also fire. "Fear candle in hay loft, in barn and in shed."

The only form of light after the sun went down was fire, and fire killed relentlessly and often. The Great Fire of London was only one example of an uncontrollable element within ordinary lives. So many other examples of death by "conflagration" existed that it seems if one survived ill-health one would as readily die of accidental burning.

But the greatest single source of superstition was the magic of religion. Throughout the whole of the Western developing world, all the way from the most ancient pagan beliefs right up to the beginning of the Americas, religion and its powerful rituals gave life to superstition.

The Blue Cloak (*Netherlandish Proverbs*) *by Pieter Breughel, 1559.*
The artist painted a visual compendium of popular folklore, rhymes and superstitions. The title is seen in the upper detail. Here, the blue cloak is a symbol for lies and deceit which the wife is hanging about her husband. The couple below pull a pretzel for luck just as we still pull the wishbone of a chicken. Such beliefs appear to die very hard.

REAL MAGIC, REAL RELIGION

THE MAGIC OF NEARLY ALL the primitive religions, from which we derive our superstitions, was a form of supernatural power which gave man the ability to control his environment. This magic was no less available in the original Christian Church. We have lost a lot of the deeper magic today, but the remnants appear each time we worry about the number 13 or whether or not we should walk under a ladder.

In simple terms, people believed that prayer worked in the same way as they had originally believed that pagan charms prevented evil spirits from damaging their lives. Witches, who behaved according to the previous belief structure by using charms and incantations, were burned at the stake once the Christians took over, but the same ideas applied. So, for saint in pre-Christian times we could read witch.

Those that would eventually become saints were in a way specialists in the same way as doctors are today (except that sainthood was granted only after death), and as witches were in pagan Europe. The line of power can be traced in this way – witch (shaman) to saint to doctor. And out of each expert within the different systems of each era came the superstitions that we still observe today.

Witch dolls and shamanic, magical, power figures. *The late 19th- century doll shown below on this page came with a written curse proving this type of magic was still being practised in Europe less than a century ago.*

SALT AND WATER

THE BASIC RITUAL within Christian belief was the benediction of salt and water for the health of the body and the expulsion of evil spirits. The liturgical books of the time also contained rituals devised to bless homes, cattle, crops, ships, tools, armor, wells, and kilns – the requirements for a stable life. All these things needed to work if an individual or a family were going to be able to survive the uncertainty of the elements and conditions that prevailed. There were special formulas that ranged across all the activities of "normal" life, from blessings for those who were preparing travel to fight battles or travel across unknown lands, right down to gathering food or moving house. There were special procedures for blessing the sick and for dealing with sick animals, for driving away thunder and for making the marriage bed fruitful.

Almost all these rituals required the presence of the appointed "power" individual. In the Christian Church this was of course the priest, whereas before Christianity it was the shaman or witch. In this century it is usually the doctor or scientist and occasionally the priest.

In today's baptism ritual within the Christian Church, the priest uses holy water and the sign of the cross to perform the process of banishing original sin, perhaps one of the most powerful remaining superstitions in the twentieth century. This exorcism was always the very foundation of superstitious belief, banishing the devil or any other potentially attendant evil spirit from some material body or object by the pronunciation of prayers and the invocation of God's name. Holy water, and originally salt, were employed generally to ward off evil and improve health, potency, and the ability to reproduce.

Every so often holy water was carried around the local parish, and pious individuals were given the opportunity to sprinkle it on their homes, their fields, their domestic animals, and anything else they considered needed it. In southern Italy and Spain today, the ritual is still employed and at the door of all Catholic churches throughout Europe and the United States there is still a font containing holy water for the crossing ritual.

The devil was allergic to holy water. This was a simple fact and much vampiric legends grow out of this belief, as we can see from the many vampire movies in which holy water seems somehow to create an enormous amount of steam and vapor in the same way as acid would if spilled on human flesh!

So, the Church was effectively a repository of supernatural power in the same way as the old pagan monuments and stone circles had been before, and the designated "officers" of this powerful center were set apart from the rest of the community, again in similar ways to the shamanic "priests", with unusual requirements such as celibacy and ritual consecration defining their position as mediators between man and God. The inevitable result of this arrangement was that there arose a cluster of popular superstitions which endowed religious devices and their users with magical powers.

Perhaps we can begin to appreciate what extraordinary times gave birth to and supported the superstitions that we are still familiar with today. The very word superstition derives from the Latin "super" meaning above, and "stare" to stand. Those that survived in battle were called "superstites," as they had outlived their fellow warriors and therefore stood above them. The superstitions that still exist today stand above the ages that

attempted to obliterate them, and therefore often seem bizarre to us because they are the remains of an age that we often know nothing else about except the superstition. But what an age that was! Filled with magic and ritual, harmony and drama, passion and power, as we shall now see.

SUPERSTITIONS

THEIR LORE
& SOURCES

Credulity, Superstition and Fanaticism *by William Hogarth 1762. British Museum Library. Here we see the savage eye of the artist showing various charlatans acting upon credulous Londoners, supported by some of the more outrageous superstitions of the time. The preacher, who is really a harlequin beneath his sacred robes, plays with a witch and a devil puppet. The devil appears again below, whispering in a sleeping man's ear while the notorious hoaxer, Mary Tofts, who claimed to have given birth to rabbits through the agency of being stared at by a buck, lies in the foreground. On the top of a thermometer of madness is an allusion to the famous, 18th century, Cock Lane Ghost while the rest of the congregation act out the most notorious cases of delusion, fraudulence and superstitions then current.*

CHAPTER ONE

A BODY OF SUPERSTITION

Left: ***Zodiacal Man and Woman*** *from the 15th c.
manuscript, Les Tres Riches Heures du Duc de Berry.*
Above: ***Zodiacal Adam*** *from 14th c. manuscript.
Bayerische Staatsbibliothek, Munich.*

THE MEDICAL BODY

THE BODY IN THE ANCIENT ENVIRONMENT of the "pagan" world was literally a mystical temple in danger of attack by demons of one sort or another. To mystics and magicians of all ages, and still today, the body is not to be taken for granted any more than the modern home or car. In fact, during the twentieth century we are just beginning again to become as aware of our bodies as we are the cars we drive them around in. We pay attention to our exercise needs, our dietary needs. In a sense we polish the surfaces of our bodies and try to make them shine.

We may not yet have taken up the complex rituals and magical rites that existed for the ancients, but we're moving that way with our aerobics, our awareness of food intake, and our daily routines for health and fitness. In fact, today most of us would acknowledge that it is foolish to smoke, drink too much alcohol, overeat, consume too many fatty foods, and not undertake a good brisk walk every other day or work out at the gym. In the same way, during the hundreds of years in which the basis for superstitions was formulated, it would have been really foolish to ignore the magical beliefs and their precepts, for these were the dominating factors of life.

Even though we may imagine we live in a more scientific age today, it is amazing how much we still pay attention to the essences of superstition and ancient mystical belief. We might not accept the dictum of "speak of the devil and he's sure to appear," but how many of us would seriously contemplate cancer as a likely disease that might attack without the underlying sense that simply in the thought we might attract it? Maybe fear of the disease increases the chance of it arriving in our bodies.

The "new age" fashion which has flourished throughout the United States has brought with it an extraordinary reversion to ancient medical cures. We commonly visit acupuncturists, faith healers, and psychic healers. We think nothing of paying attention to homeopathic cures and natural remedies, most of which take their source from ancient herbal medicines and even incantations and rituals. Modern doctors in this century have largely removed the concept of self-cure from humanity, but the human attitude toward the medical profession derives its awe-inspired sense to the ignorance of the sufferer rather than a greater degree of medical understanding. We still feel the same way about our witchdoctors and healers, even though we now attribute a more rational source to their activities.

On the simplest, most superficial level, how about sneezing?

Why do we so readily say "bless you" when others sneeze? What possible danger could there be from a simple sneeze?

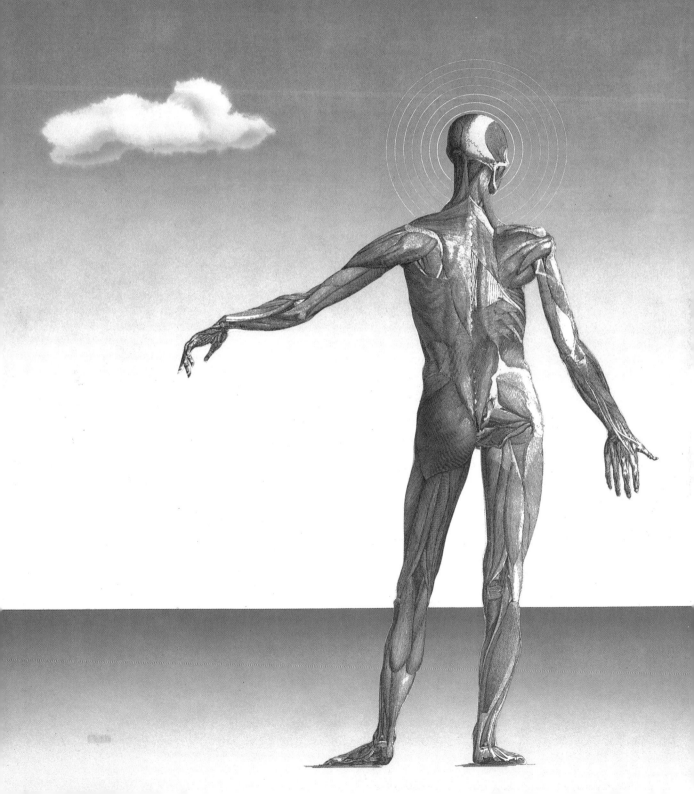

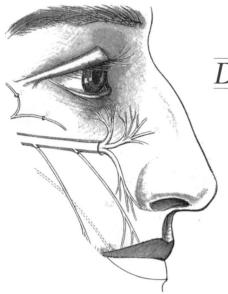

DIVINE SNEEZE

Sneezing was also common among sufferers of the bubonic plague during the Middle Ages in Europe, and so the custom of blessing the sneezer continues to this day as a worthy precaution.

Superstition

When someone sneezes, we say "Bless you."

Lore and Sources

Tiberius Caesar in AD 150 would ride around in his chariot and shout "Bless you" to any member of the public that sneezed, and "Bless you, bless you my dear" to the second and third sneezes. Evidently the offer of blessing arose from a serious disease that attacked the early Romans in which sneezing was the main symptom. Sufferers frequently died as a result, although it was believed that the more blessings offered, the less likely was the chance of death.

It was also thought to be a form of well-wishing. "God Bless you" and "God keep you" were offerings of good health and care to those that sneezed.

The old word for sneezing was "sternutation" According to the ancient mythology, when the god Prometheus made the first man from clay he immediately started sneezing (suffering from sternutation) because Prometheus had stolen the celestial fire from the sun to make the first man and apparently a cold in the nose was the result. The ancient Gentiles therefore worshipped the sneezer.

"If you sneeze on a Monday, you sneeze for danger;

Sneeze on a Tuesday, kiss a stranger;

Sneeze on a Wednesday, sneeze for a letter;

Sneeze on a Thursday, something better;

Sneeze on a Friday, sneeze for sorrow;

Sneeze on a Saturday, see your sweetheart tomorrow.

Sneeze on a Sunday, and the devil will have domination over you all week!"

God would certainly need to bless the hay-fever sufferer!

CROSSING THE FACE

Superstition

Placing a hand in front of the face when yawning.

Lore and Sources

Is it simply politeness and the desire not to spread "germs," that causes us to place the hand before the face or is there a deeper significance?

According to "Sperenza" Wilde in her book *Superstitions of Ireland*, making the sign of the cross before the mouth when yawning prevented the devil from rushing into the body and taking up residence there. Presumably he would slip around from the back where he was normally in residence, avoiding flying salt, and run down the throat! Mothers would close the baby's mouth, or make the cross before it when it yawned, for fear of the devil taking over the innocent young. Today's covering of the mouth derives from this.

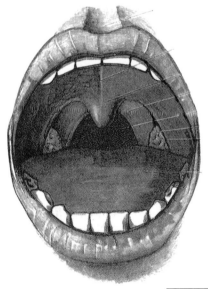

*A **Demon** from the Bohemian Codex Gigas, 13th.c.*

SHOULD-I-SHUDDER-WHEN-A-SHADOW-SHOWETH-DEATH

Superstition

Fear of shadows.

Lore and Sources

And at the end of the day when the yawning has persuaded you that it is time to go to sleep, look out for the shadows on the wall cast by the flickering log fires. If you see a shadow without a head, it means that the person casting it will die before the next Christmas Eve. Christmas was the Christian deadline but in earlier times other celestial or seasonal dates would have been used, such as the end of Fall and the coming of the new year.

The shadow, in fact, occupies an important part of superstition in relation to the body because its presence or absence was originally connected to very deep religious and pagan beliefs. Remember Peter Pan's lack of a shadow?

The most ancient understanding of the body and soul was that the soul was attached to the body in such a way that under certain circumstances it could be removed and would thereafter drift away as the soul on its way to afterlife. If a vampire came up behind you and nailed your shadow to the wall, it took possession of your body. If some poor unfortunate died in the night and the shadow/soul drifted away, there was danger that it would cross water and be unable to reach the afterlife. Instead it would go back into the dead body and become the "undead" or the "walking dead," a form of vampire. This gave rise to the habit of putting lids on rain-water barrels and gave added significance to bridges.

The work of the northern artist Edvard Munch often shows the long raking shadows so unique to the Scandinavian landscape. They seem to be as alive as the sitters, ominously surrounding each figure like the dark fears which emanate from superstitious beliefs.

CURIOUS CURES AND OLD WIVES' TALES

NOT ALL SUPERSTITIONS surrounding the body were involved in religious themes such as these. Many of them were direct "cures" that came from beliefs brought about by "old wives' tales."

Throughout the coming pages we will come across old wives' tales again and again, so it's worth a brief look at the "old wife" herself, for curiously she actually did exist.

Even today there are still living representatives of an ancient rural healer in existence. Originally she occupied various specialist positions within a community, such as wart-healer, herbalist, tooth-puller, blood-charmer, bone-setter, and general "quack-doctor." Presumably the bone-setter was brought in after the tooth-puller had dislocated the patient's shoulder attempting to remove an offending tooth. The quack-doctor was originally named the "quack-salver," the name derived from the words "quacken", meaning one who talked pretentiously about his or her expert knowledge, and "salve", meaning a kind of cure.

The range covered by these "specialists" extended not only to general cures of the body but also psychological therapies, emotional disorders, and beauty treatments derived from supernatural sources such as washing the face with dew gathered on May Day morning or the use of urine as a skin lotion!

One of the most notorious genuine doctors of the past, Michel de Nostradamus (sixteenth century), was not only a full-fledged physician, qualified from Montpellier University in France, but an amazing preparer of delicious marmalades and jams, a beauty therapist who created creams and salves for women, and an alchemist. This unlikely combination of expertise was perfectly common from the Middle Ages right up to the end of the nineteenth century, as life was seen as a flow of understanding connected to the natural elements provided by Mother Nature in her bountiful abilities.

Such healers, or old wives, also provided attendant incantations to be spoken during the cures, for example for a painful burn or scald from hot water the following lines, which have no traceable source, would have been spoken:

"There came three angels out of the West,
One brought fire and the other brought frost.
In the name of the Father, Son and Holy Ghost,
Out fire . . . in frost."

Right: *The healer **Saint Lucy** by Francesco del Cossa. This is the Christianized version of the Sabine goddess, Lucetia, who was the great Mother of Light. Tuscan witches still use Lucina's healing chain which is a wreath of rue tied with a ribbon. The patient must spit three times upon the wreath, calling on St Lucy for protection against the evil eye.*

*The boy child with a dog is a very emotive image. Not only does the seventh child of a seventh child have second sight but their dog companions are believed to be able to see ghosts and beings from the Otherworld. Male 'seers' are more likely to have a dog as familiar than they are a cat. Below: Families in the mid 19th-century invariably were large enough to support seventh children so second sight was not the rare occurrence that it might be today. Below left: **Charles French** c.1832 by Asahel Powers. Right: **Boy and Dog** by Noah North, Rockefeller Folk Art Center.*

Superstition

A seventh child possesses special powers.

Certain qualifications were essential to the healer's art. Being the seventh daughter of a seventh daughter (or seventh son of a seventh son) brought the power to heal by touch especially if the parents had been seventh children. Seven was accepted as the most sacred of numbers, and seventh children possessed "second sight" and the art of seeing the future. Although today it is not so common to find a family with as many as seven children, until the end of the Victorian era huge families were very common. Another reason presumably, why there are so few mystics around in the latter part of the twentieth century!

Lore and Sources

The only source that makes any clear practical sense with regard to seventh children, apart from the sacredness of the number seven, is that large families originally selected the seventh child to become a doctor as a matter of tradition (the child was known as the Septimus child). Thus science and religion were brought together in a way that is rarely the case today.

Superstition

Each finger has special significance and can be used for certain cures or magic.

In matters of rural healing, fingers were thought to be of the greatest significance for treating cuts and sore places on the body of humans and animals, whether by professional healers or laymen.

Lore and Sources

The third finger of the left hand was known as the "medical finger" and during the Middle Ages physicians used only this finger to stir medicines. If there was any poison present in the medicine, using this finger was said to prompt the heart into missing a beat because it was the only finger connected directly to the heart by a single nerve, thus the use of this finger to carry the wedding ring.

Conversely, the forefinger of the right hand was known to be the poison finger and could never be used to apply ointments to wounds or to aid any healing, as it was known throughout Europe to be the "witch finger," the lethal indicating finger used by a witch to throw black magic at her victims.

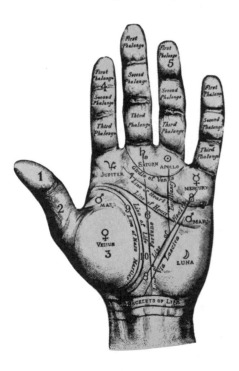

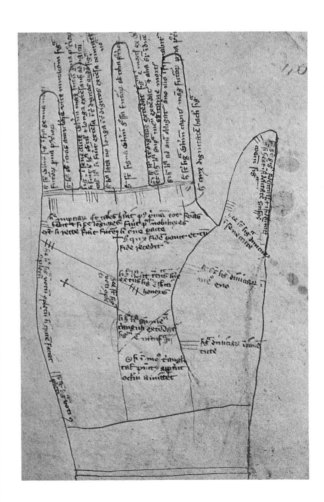

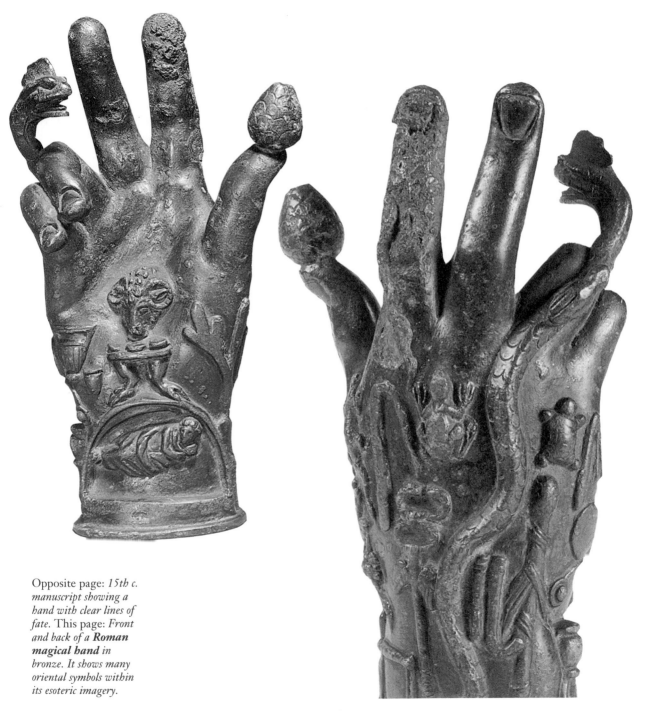

Opposite page: *15th c. manuscript showing a hand with clear lines of fate.* This page: *Front and back of a **Roman magical hand** in bronze. It shows many oriental symbols within its esoteric imagery.*

THE BODY AND THE PLANETS

THE VILLAGE WISE WOMAN also carried the power to rule the planets and thus carried forward the most ancient astrological doctrines that each part of the body is under the jurisdiction of a particular star.

*Astrological sign of the Scorpion. From the 13th c. Persian Book of the Stars. Often the remarkable sciences and astronomical knowledge of the Islamic Arabs of the 10th and 11th centuries found their way into mediaeval Europe in such distorted forms they ended up as superstitions. The illustration on the opposite page shows a 15th-century **zodiacal man** from the Guildbook of Barber Surgeons of York.*

Saturn governed the bladder, bones, spleen, and "circulating juices."

Jupiter governed the bile, kidneys, veins, and sexual organs.

Venus governed the uterus, breasts, spermatic tubes, loins, and buttocks.

Mercury governed the memory, imagination, brain, and all mental processes, the hands, feet, legs and bile.

The Sun governed the brain, nerves, urine, right eye of a man, and the left eye of a woman, and the optic nerves.

The Moon governed the mouth, brain, belly, intestines, the organs of reproduction, the left eye of a male and the right eye of a female, the female liver, and the left side of the body.

The Sun and the Moon were seen as opposites and therefore governed opposites in the body.

Based on these astrological and astronomical concepts, cures for corns on the feet, for example, had to be applied at the moment of a shooting star. Given the rhythms of the world and an understanding of the elements, one could dislodge a fishbone from the throat only while the feet were plunged in ice-cold water. To cure a headache one was obliged to pour vinegar onto a door hinge, and the cure for toothache was facilitated by holding garlic in the palm of the hand.

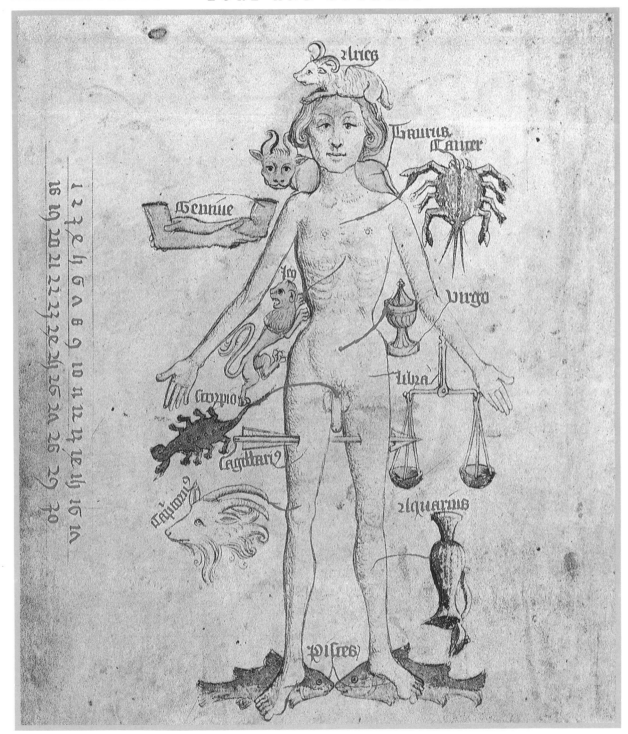

THE MAGICIAN HEALER IN AMERICA

THE EUROPEAN "OLD WIFE" was not the only one to provide power and magic for the superstitious individual. The traditional magician healer thrived in the United States until far later than in England and most of Europe. In the Ozarks, for example, the "Power Doctor" healed through touch on record as late as the 1920s.

Superstition

Laying on of hands and spiritual cures can be invoked by gifted healers.

The process involved placing the hands over the affected area of the body, accompanied by a violent shivering. The ailment was thus temporarily transferred to the healer, who then quickly touched a tree to pass the sickness into the body of the trunk. The tree was felt to be able to lose the resulting sickness into the ground through its greater earthing.

Lore and Sources

For sure the source that gave individuals the power to heal with the hands came originally from the shamanic healers of early Europe and perhaps even before that from the African witch-doctor who would use his hands as medical tools. Witchcraft in the Middle Ages also employed healing methods using hands and, as we have seen, fingers. The tree as an aid for sending the ailment or any evil to earth, derives from the Celtic belief that trees were the temples of holiness and possessed the greatest represen- tation of earthly power available

Self portrait *by Henry Church, 1880. Collection of Samuel and Angela Rosenburg. This highly original spiritualist, healer, blacksmith and artist is shown with his muses which even include a smith.*

to mankind. For the Celts living throughout Europe at the time of the Romans, tree arbors were the churches of their worship.

Boils were healed by the use of spittle and the incantation, "What I see increase, what I rub decrease," repeated over and over again. The process was to be performed at the time of a waning moon. Burns were cured by blowing upon them and chanting the following well-known English charm:

> "One little Indian, two little Indians,
> One named East, one named West,
> The Son and Father and the Holy Ghost
> Ask it all in Jesus' name. Amen."

Poster advertisment *by Henry Church, 1865 Courtesy Samuel Rosenburg. Superstition and folk art combine in this early New World advertisment.*

The Amish in Pennsylvania still paint mystical symbols on their farm doors to keep away evil spirits who cause diseases.

Faith healing in the United States has gained enormous popularity in the last few decades and forms a major part of the religious environment today. The laying on of hands still comes from the same sources that were believed to be effective hundreds of years ago and is attached in the same way to a belief in God and primitive ritual, and therefore to Earth and the world in which we live. The "priest" is once again the witchdoctor or shaman, and the source of power lies in the hands of the adept in the same way as the old wife or magical healer. To this extent superstition in its purest and most practical form is alive and well in America.

OLD CURES DON'T DIE

GIVEN THE TWENTIETH CENTURY tendency to return to ancient cures and superstitions, it is fascinating to take a closer look at some of the specifics, for in doing so we find an extraordinary number of good reasons why we have never managed to kill them off – reasons indeed why we should not wish to do so.

Sicknesses known today to be caused by the transfer of bacteria or virus, such as measles or mumps, were originally believed to be caused by the possession of the body by demons.

Demons could successfully be banished only if there was someone else into which they could be transferred. This fitted well with the general propensity of disease insofar as sicknesses generally did move from one person to another and very often the original sufferer would get better once the sickness has passed on.

There are all sorts of superstitions within the medical profession today that have their sources soundly based in the past.

Superstition

Pills and capsules be given particular colors.

The original rituals that existed between physician and patient still dictate our choices of colors, particularly where physical health is concerned.

Lore and Sources

We will rarely see black pills because of the color's associations with death. Iron pills are frequently red because of the connection with blood, and pink pills are kept aside for young people whose physical development is retarded, "pink pills for pale people."

Superstition

Danger in floating spirits.

Nurses under a misconceived notion, will close hospital windows at night in order to prevent demons from entering.

Lore and Sources

Since time immemorial, mankind has believed that the body was not merely a physical presence on earth but a spiritual presence in the universe. All the major religions have encompassed this understanding in some form and the ancient, pagan and primitive peoples of Europe and America based their entire concept of life and death upon the presence of the human spirit. And just as there were good and bad living humans, so there were also good and bad spirits. The central issue surrounding the superstitions relating to vampires is that the unfortunate victim who falls prey to the undead will die in physical terms but the spirit that was supposed, under normal conditions, to float away to heaven or hell, will return to the body and bring it back to life falsely. In order to make sure that spirits did not stray accidently back into dead bodies, the ancients took all manner of precautions. Disembodied shadow/souls may be unable to find their way to the afterlife, and so could drift in through open windows. Water was believed to be a danger to departing spirits because they could drown in it, so that water barrels were covered with wooden lids (and still are today) to allow the spirit to pass by unhindered.

Superstition

Blankets in places of sickness.

Nurses making beds must never place the blankets over a chair or they endanger their patients, who will inevitably die in threes.

Lore and Sources

The dead, in the distant past, were invariably wrapped in blankets before burial, so that to leave blankets lying about the sick persons room was inviting death. The significance of the number three was related to various magical numbers, as we shall see later in the book. Multiples of three were thought to be the most fortunate or unfortunate according to the situation.

Interior with Flowers by Horace Pippin, Philadelphia Museum of Art.

Superstition

Flowers should not remain in a hospital ward at night.

Inside modern hospitals and in nursing homes there are a plethora of superstitions employed on a regular basis. Who dares keep flowers in a ward at night? The belief, quite wrongly, is that they use up valuable oxygen in the air and therefore deprive the ailing patients.

Lore and Sources

This old wives' tale derives from the belief that flowers sometimes house demons who emerge at night and attack the sick who are not strong enough to fight them off. The belief in the power of demons to possess all manner of different natural vegetation such as trees, flowers, rivers and fields, derives from the pagan concept that everything in existence was part of a a kind of magical, religious conspiracy – i.e. everything had its own appropriate god, goddess or spirit. Different forms of nature were both protected by named spirits or in danger of being attacked by them, depending on the situation or the requirement of Superstition. This most ancient of ancient beliefs comes down to us today in the form of the fear of having flowers in the presence of the sick at night.

HAIROSCOPES AND THE HAIR-AFTER

Superstition

Hair-length and its associations.

Hair is another of those entirely human phenomena that has attracted numerous beliefs both for and against lengthy locks. Samson aided the story by his support of the connection between long hair and strength while the 1960s and early 1970s promoted all manner of conflicts between the social view of hair length and the rebellious young. The progression into the 1980s and 1990s has seen the advent of the "businessman" culture in which success and social adherence has persuaded men into wearing their hair short again. Long hair can be degenerate or it can be artistic and expressive. It can be effeminate or virile. Eric Maple states in his book *Superstitions and the Superstitious* that the length of hair "is in effect merely a twentieth-century contradictory superstition which asks us to believe that the strength of the state and the stability of society generally is in some unexplained way dependent upon the length of hair worn by its citizens."

Lore and Sources

Shorn locks have been employed for hundreds of years in all sorts of ways for the benefit of magic rituals. It was believed that to keep cut hair invited sickness. Baldness could be cured by positive thinking or determined prayer, and there are even astrological experts in the United States offering special hair-styles allied to personal horoscopes, known as "hairoscopes!" Hair was originally associated with power and good health or vitality and virility or fertility. The early Viking people in Europe wore their hair constantly long with thick beard growths, because, very simply, this kept them warm in the harsh climates of the north. The American Indian still today retains long hair because of the original associations with strength.

If we go back still further in time, to the very earliest origins of human beings, there are conjectures amongst modern anthropologists that women would grow their hair long because of the need to retreat into water with their children to escape from preying animals. The child would float beside the standing mother and hold onto the long tresses of hair.

1. SHOCK-HEADED PETER.

Just look at him! There he stands,
With his nasty hair and hands.
See! his nails are never cut;
They are grim'd as black as soot;
And the sloven, I declare,
Never once has comb'd his hair;
Any thing to me is sweeter
Than to see Shock-headed Peter.   (2)

Left: **The English Struwwelpeter**; or Pretty stories and funny pictures for little children by Dr. Heinrich Hoffman. The Gothic, German imagery was hardly what might be, even generously, called pretty. The curious moral book found greater favor with parents than it did with their poor, code-bound children. Below: **Punk hairstyles**, London, 1990.

CURES AND CHARMS

WARTABILITY

Superstition

The curing of warts.

Warts have helped retain one of the most successful areas of superstitious cure, largely because the original methods, still not understood by modern medicine, appear to be amongst the few that actually work.

The old cures, described as a "judicious mixture of spittle and muttered charms" are actually far more effective in their results than this unfair description might imply.

Lore and Sources

Love Spoons
During the last two centuries it was a widespread custom in Wales for young men to carve elaborate love tokens for their beloveds in the form of wooden spoons. And just as warts are charmed by hazelwood, each "love wood" was chosen to enhance fertility, sexual attraction or faithfulness. The young woman would then use the spoon for mixing her own love potions to strengthen the bond.

Warts were "charmed" by notching a hazel stick and rubbing it onto the wart, though an important part of the cure was to forget about it after the charm was effected. Or you could rub a piece of raw meat onto the wart and then bury the meat – as the meat decays so the wart is charmed. Another method was to count each wart and then forget the counting.

Touching the warts with a pebble and then leave the pebble at a crossroads. The unfortunate person who picks up the pebbles and examines them takes on the warts! This one undoubtedly adhered to the passing on of sickness ritual that applied to viruses. Of all the wart charms, the most popular and effective seems to be the purchase of a wart from a child for a silver coin.

But there is one important rule to all this, perhaps the reason wart charmers invariably remain unknown, and that is that the charmers and their cures remain secret and silent. The more they are advertised the less effective the charms. The publication and reading of this book could do untold harm to wart charming, so remember, don't tell anyone!

In the 18th-Century
apothecaries were permitted to
act as doctors. Many offered a
more questionable trade in
potions and remedies for
anything from warts to
unrequited love.

P:
MUMIÆ.

Extr.
G.Opii

Melissa

AQ
ABSYNTI

Extr:
Helleb:
Nig:

ANCIENT CURES AND CAUSES

Virgin & Child by Carlo Crivelli, V & A Museum, London. The Christ Child carries the apple from Eden, redeeming the Original Sin.

ANCIENT CURES FOR AND CAUSES OF SICKNESS come in all sorts of different forms, handed down to us by old wives and quacks, some with a remarkable degree of good sense, and others without any sense at all. It seems proper to devote a part of the book to some of the worthy and less worthy superstitious cures and causes that we have inherited, though as always with the "medical" aspect of this

book, extreme caution is recommended in the application of them. There are numerous reports on record of proponents suffering horrendous results and even death from the use of so-called health aids of this kind. Though one could, of course, add that within the sophisticated and advanced cures of modern medicine there are daily disasters incurred by the application of the cures proposed by modern physicians also! So it is probably better not to take this list too seriously and certainly better not to try any of the cures or believe in any of the causes yourself.

Superstition

Appendicitis can be caused by swallowing orange seeds (or any kind of seed).

Source

The origin of this belief was that the seed would somehow become embedded in the appendix and therefore cause eventual swelling.

Superstition

An apple a day keeps the doctor away.

Source

The apple fruit has been an important part of the most ancient folk-lore ever since the Bible told of how Adam and Eve ate from the Tree of the Knowledge of Good and Evil. Apple trees have ever since been considered as almost sacred items of nature and modern gardeners will rarely be willing to uproot an apple orchard as it is considered sacrilege to do so. Undoubtedly the origin of this belief is, in turn, rooted in the Celtic beliefs that we have already seen.

Crossroads on Dartmoor.
*Charmers still flourish to this
day in the moorlands of South
Western England. Many are
highly regarded by doctors
and vets alike. How these,
often simple and
unpretentious, country folk
manage to heal ailments as
different as migraine in
children to ringworm in cows
remains unknown. But they
are as likely to use an
irrational method, like
leaving a pebble or stone by a
crossroads to relieve the
sufferer of warts, as any
superstitious housewife of
three centuries ago.*

Superstition

Asthma can be relieved by eating lots of carrots.

Source

Carrots were amongst the most readily available root vegetables in Europe during the Middle Ages and were attributed with numerous curing powers, including the ability to give good sight in darkness. Asthma was associated with a general weakness of body and spirit so that the vitality of the carrot was thought to bring back the missing energy.

Superstition

Boils can be cured by keeping a nutmeg in the pocket.

Source

Nutmeg is a natural hallucinogen if taken in appropriate, very large quantities. It is said that the famous 16th century prophet Nostradamus was often under its influence while making his predictions. Nutmeg, in any event, was commonly employed in witchcraft for its powerful curative powers and today, used in small measure, it acts as a pleasant food additive. There is no accessible source to tell us why a nutmeg in the pocket should have any effect on boils, except where a powerful white magic incantation had been additionally employed to release believed magical powers.

Superstition

Arthritis can be cured by the application of boiled sting-ing nettles.

Source

The liquid dropped by the stinging nettle onto the unsuspecting country rambler is a powerful irritant. It was originally believed that this liquid contained natural muscle relaxants which would aid the pain caused by arthritic suffering. As with most of these natural cures, someone at some time must have been cured this way and the story got around.

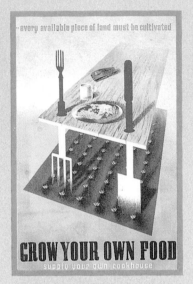

During World War II there was strict
rationing of food in the UK. The
Ministry of Agriculture campaigned
for home grown produce to help the
food shortages and especially
recommended carrots as containing a
substance which supposedly improved
vision at night. This would have been
very useful during the enforced
blackouts. However the Nazis became
convinced that the British had some
secret weapon for seeing at night.
Although carrots are an extremely
healthy food there is little scientific
evidence to suggest an enhancement of
the eyecones.

Superstition

Deadly diseases can be given to a child by a cat sucking its breath.

Source

There is still today a strong association between cats and ancient witchcraft. But cats have been the familiars of those that perform magic since long before medieval witchcraft was born, as far back as Egyptian times. Particularly black cats were thought to be possessed of special powers which helped the magician, or later the witch, perform magical tasks, black being associated with the power of death. The source, as we shall see later in the book in the section concerned with animal superstitions, is probably based in vampirism and the sucking of the spirit or life from the defenceless body.

Superstition

Long before science agreed, it was believed that burns and scalds are reduced in intensity by plunging the burned part of the skin into cold water.

Source

It is now understood by medical science that when a burn occurs, the blood rushes to the damaged spot and increases the intensity of the heat, which in turn worsens the burn. The cold water reduces the temperature of the skin and blood and so tends to reduce the degree of the burn itself. Here then we have a perfect example of an old superstition being approved by modern science.

Left: ***Portrait of a little girl*** *1969 by Fred Aris, courtesy of the Portal Gallery.* Below: ***Rosa Gallica Officialis*** *from Mary Lawrence's "A collection of Roses from Nature".*

Superstition

The brain may be kept clear by sprinkling the eyebrows with rosewater.

Source

Rosewater was made from the gathering of large quantities of rose petals, which were then fermented and infused. The result was a very high concentration of vitamin C, though in ancient Europe, the significance of this vitamin was not specifically known. The result of applying either rosewater or crushed rose petals which had been dried and then put beneath the tongue, was a real cure for various infections, one of which might have been believed to be a head cold. Bubonic plague was successfully cured in Southern France during the mid-sixteenth century using rose capsules placed under the tongue.

Above: ***Gathering in Bulgaria*** for attar of roses. Below: ***Sorting roses*** for perfume in Grasse, France. From the Illustrated London News, 1891. Invariably it is the rose which forms the basis of most 19th and 20th century perfumes.

Superstition

Corns on the feet can be cured by taking some brown paper, soaking it in vinegar, and placing it in a saucer under the bed. Dab the corn with saliva each day before breakfast, or dissolve a pearl button in lemon juice and dab it on the corn night and morning.

Source

Even as recently as the 1950s, mothers in parts of Southern Europe would wrap a child's wound in vinegar and brown paper. The vinegar, with its acidic qualities, would help to dry out the wound,

and the brown paper acted as an absorbent. Vinegar also gives off a strong smell and was originally thought, therefore, to act upon the corn overnight, the odour was thought to be a kind of essence that rose from the soaked brown paper into the corn and thus tenderized it.

Saliva has a whole history of its own within superstitious lore. Spitting into the hand was originally believed, as long ago as AD 77, to create greater force to any effort because it made the hand heavier and therefore the effort greater, whatever the intention. Professional fist-fighters would spit into the hand in order to increase the force of the blow upon the adversary. Even today we might see a strong-armed man spit into his hand before taking a hammer to strike a stake into the ground.

Spitting also helped to send away the devil, in the same way as throwing salt over the shoulder, spitting in the same direction could also be employed, though to somewhat messier results! Most bars in the ancient American West were equipped with spittoons to facilitate this somewhat unsavory habit.

The earliest available sources of saliva as a cure come from the beginning of the first century AD and, during the centuries that

followed, old wives, witches, and wizards employed spittle, usually from a person that had fasted for at least a few days, and applied it to cure all sorts of ailments, including cuts, sores, and even birthmarks. The saliva of one that had fasted was believed to contain a greater amount of salt, and as we will see later in the book (Salt Superstitions), salt was considered to be the purest of substances.

The pearl button dissolved in lemon juice constitutes a complex mixture of superstition and chemistry. The pearl was believed to represent human tears which also contained a high level of salt. The transfer that was somehow enacted between the salty tears and the pearl button defies

reason, but perhaps pearls and the acidity of lemon juice had some softening effect on the corns.

Circus poster Germany 1900. *The perfect image of the strong man protected by his tattoos. It is perhaps surprising to see even young boys of today spitting on their hands before attempting a challenging physical task. Like many superstitions it is become such an accepted custom that few would ever think of commenting upon it, let alone wonder how it came about.*

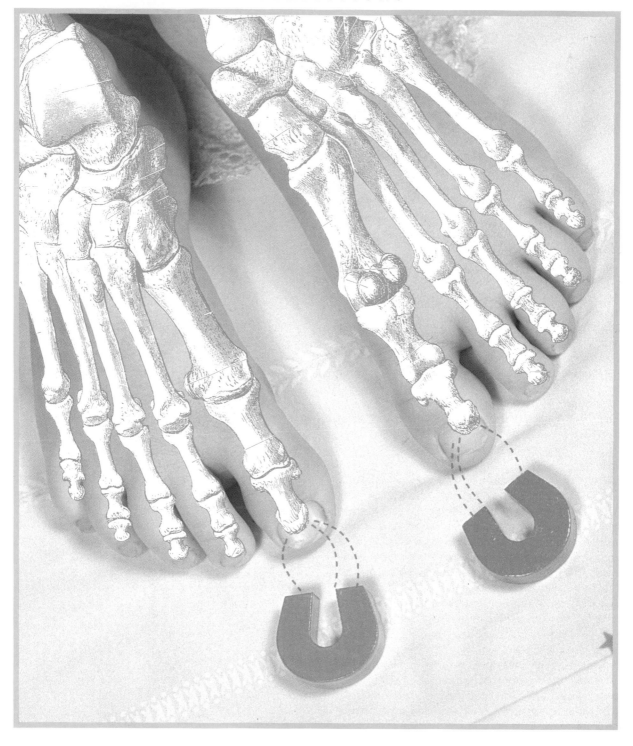

Superstition

Cramp can be cured by keeping a magnet at the bottom of the bed, the prongs directed towards the feet. The magnetism will draw out the pain. Alternatively wear a "tarred yarn" around the upper leg as a garter.

Source

Magnetic force, once science understood it to be connected to the earth's natural energies, was employed to draw out sickness, particularly that associated with muscular problems. There was no effective truth in the idea whatever.

The second cure for cramp within this superstition, of putting a "tarred yarn" around the leg, on the other hand, carries within it one of the most ancient derivations. Tarred yarn was either a piece of very strong string or rope, covered in tar (water-proof, carbon-based coating), and used by fishermen, or a thinner material used for knitting, also coated in a thick sticky black liquid.

Winding thread has its own extensive history, and anyone who has watched a grandmother or old aunt wind a ball of wool from another's out-stretched hands, also watches the holiest of super-stitions being enacted. The earliest origin was the process of making thread on a spinning wheel, stretching out the wool or yarn from the natural fiber and then spinning it into a strong thread to be used for making cloth. In children's fairy tales, such as *Sleeping Beauty*, the old bad witch uses the needle of the spinning wheel to cast a spell upon the innocent princess, who then sleeps for a hun-dred years. Spinning wheels were considered to be possessed of great magical power and so the thread that they made was also endowed with energy for either curing or causing sickness.

The tar's capacity to help facilitate the cure of cramp derived from the good fortune that fisherman were considered to possess, for it was fishermen that employed tar most commonly for their work. Tar also happened to contain large quantities of carbon which may have had some curative effect.

Below: *Mesmerists of the 18th century believed that they could use 'an animal magnetism' to change the energies in the body and thus bring about a healing process.*

Superstition

Fever may be abated by drinking boiled onions or alter-natively by carrying a key in the palm of the hand.

Source

Boiled onions do actually have a curative effect on high temperature in some cases, depending on the source of the fever, so that this old wives' tale has some grounding in medicine. Boiling and eating onions is said to stimulate the liver and enhance the blood circulation, which in turn helps the stomach to function more efficiently. Carrying a key in the palm of the hand, conversely, only derived its power from an idea. In most medieval home medicine, cure was believed to be facilitated by transference of the sickness, either into another person or an item such as a tree, a flower, or in this case, a key. The key was particularly significant because it unlocked or locked things and thus was connected with security.

Superstition

Gout may be cured by walking barefoot in dewy grass.

Source

Dew was sent by God, or before Christianity, the gods or sprites of the early morning, and therefore contained purity and curative abilities. Gout affected the legs and feet and so the connection was obvious!

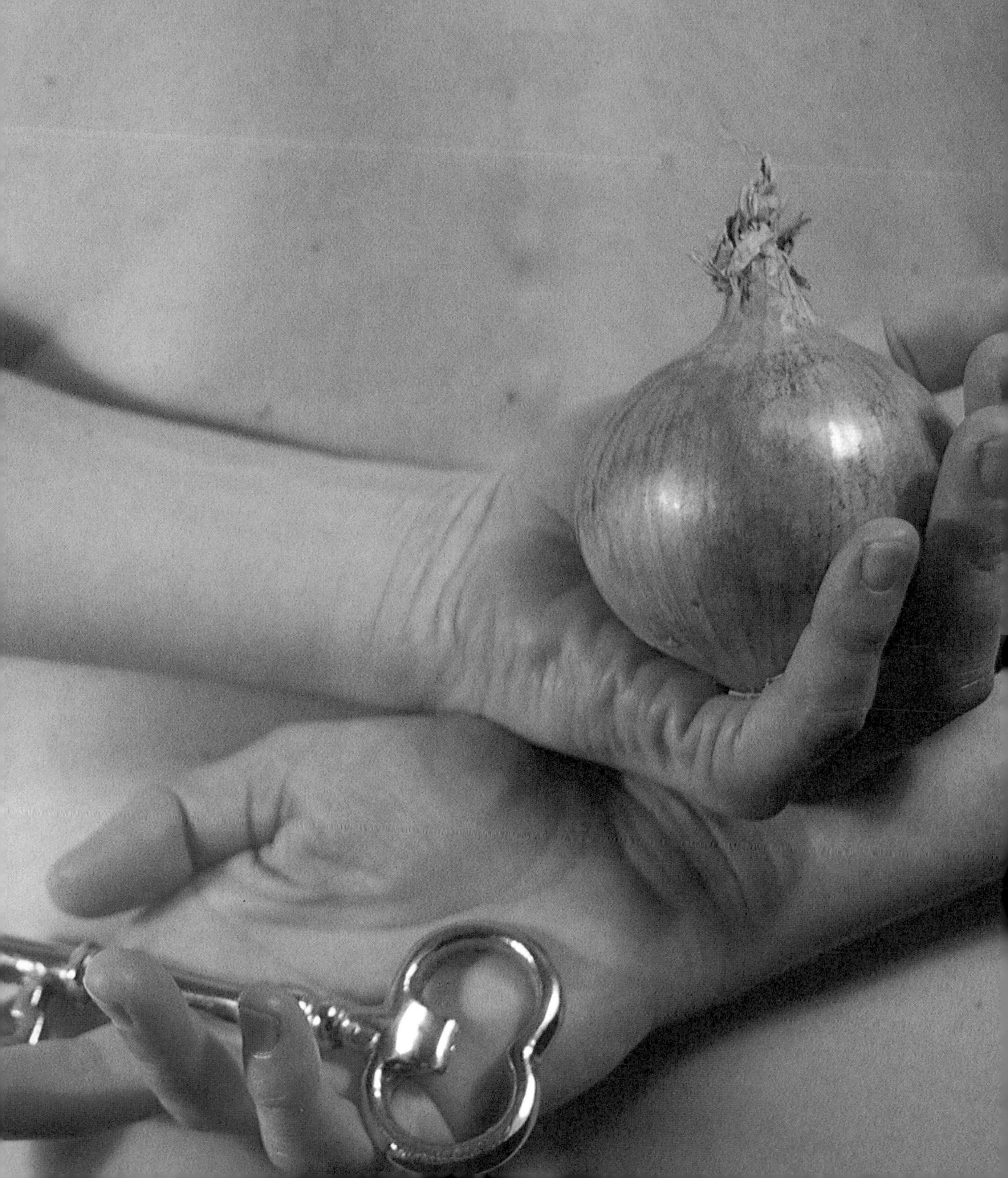

Superstition

Headaches could be cured by many different methods, some more bizarre than others. To provide all the methods would almost fill a whole book on its own, so that just a few of the more interesting ones are provided here.

An onion rubbed over the aching area will stop the pain. Ice in a pack placed over the offending part of the head or placing the head under a cold-water shower will stop the ache. The juice of the celery vegetable will cure a headache derived from indigestion.

Above: **Stone operation** by *Hieronymus Bosch, Prado, Madrid.* Right: *Trephaning or perforation of the skull. Miniature from Vigeviono's work on anatomy dated 1345.*

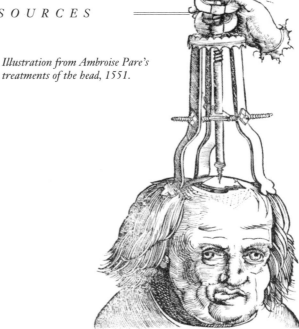

Illustration from Ambroise Pare's treatments of the head, 1551.

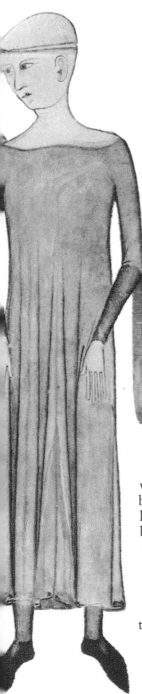

Sources

Once again onions do have a curative power. However, rubbing an onion on the surface of the skin would not seem to be greatly effective, though the original idea was based in the root quality of the onion – "close to earth, close to cure."

Reducing the temperature of the head by using ice or cold water derived from the belief that pain was related to heat. The heat that was very often felt around an area of pain was actually the preponderance of blood at the sight of injury or infection, and this was transferred onto body pains also. The cold water would banish the heat of the blood and therefore temporarily reduce the sense of pain, but shortly after the ice was removed, the pain would return, so that the remedy would not work for long.

Celery juice does cure a headache caused by indigestion as celery contains high alkaline and will therefore counteract the excess of acidity brought about by poor eating habits.

Superstition

That a headache may be cured by driving a nail into the skull.

Source

Ivan the Terrible was said to have ordered nails to be driven into the heads of his courtiers if they complained of headaches. During the late seventeenth century the medical profession adopted a cure, called "trephaning", which was composed of cutting a hole in the side of the skull, often as large as a coin, and allowing the skin to grow over it. Documented results show some degree of success, though failures are less spoken of. Even in the last fifty years, the medical process of "lobotomy" entailed the driving of a long metal pin into the frontal lobe of the brain, skewering it about in a clockwise motion and then pulling it out again. The "cure" was applied to particularly extreme mental patients and was said to "calm them down". It also very often either killed them or turned them into permanent vegetables.

In ancient Rome and Egypt the same idea was applied, and the superstition of curing a headache by driving a nail into the skull derives from this. Incidentally, it doesn't work!

Superstition

Lockjaw can be brought about by cutting the ligament between the thumb and forefinger.

Source

Probably understood to be the case because carpenters and joiners were frequently having this accident and allowing the wound to becoming septic and septisemia causes lockjaw.

Superstition

Heart disease may be cured by drinking foxglove tea.

Source

The drinking of foxglove tea as a cure for heart problems is older than witchcraft itself, and has continued until this day, largely because it appear to work. Medicine, during the past half century has adopted the foxglove's natural properties in the preparation of the medicine "digitalis," which is extensively used in the relief of heart disease. It is advised, that before undertaking any such curative methods, the reader should consult a doctor.

Superstition

Cures for hiccups.

Everyone has their own personal cure for hiccups, and most are familiar to us today, such as drinking out of a full glass of water from the back of the glass or having someone make us jump from a big shock. Perhaps the most common is holding the breath for as long as possible. A more religious method might be to say "ave maria" ten times. All these cures relate to one central issue – controlling or changing the pattern of the breath, and therefore the fluctuations of the diaphragm that cause hiccups. These superstitious cures all derive from our distant past, though their original form was different.

Source

From the seventeenth century in England – repeat three times while holding the breath:
"Hiccup, sniccup, look up, right up,
Three drops in a cup, good for the hiccup."

Left: *Ancient Britons under a sacred oak from an 18th century print. The oak, the sickle, mistletoe and acorns all had ritual significance and many of these rites and themes survive as superstitions in modern folklore. We will still say "Touch wood" even when we have long forgotten the original sacred meaning for doing so.* Below: *Of all the trees in northern Europe the oak seems to have had pride of sanctity. Drawing by William Clark, Victoria and Albert Museum Library, London.*

Superstition

Lumbago (a painful form of back rheumatism)can be cured by rolling about in grass at the sound of the first cuckoo.

Source

Grass at the time of the sound of the first cuckoo is covered with dew, and dew, as we discovered in the cure for gout, contains the nectar of the gods. The first cuckoo sings in Spring, therefore bringing fresh life with the first season of the year (in harvest terms).

Superstition

Mental disorders will become worse at full moon.

Source

The moon has long been associated with human mental problems, both positively and negatively. The full moon could bring good fortune or bad, sanity and insanity. The original source probably derives from the qualities of the moon in ancient mythology, which were associated with imbalance and fear. The name "lunatic" was awarded to those whom it was believed went crazy, or became more crazy, during full moon nights. It was also believed that violently insane people would turn into werewolves during the full moon period.

Superstition

Night air is dangerous to health, so keep the windows closed at night.

Source

This is related once again to the vampiric lore of the ancient past, as far back as ancient Egypt, where spirits were believed to need a clear, open and benevolent route to the afterlife. Leaving windows open at night encouraged passing spirits to enter and take up residence in the sleeping occupant of the room.

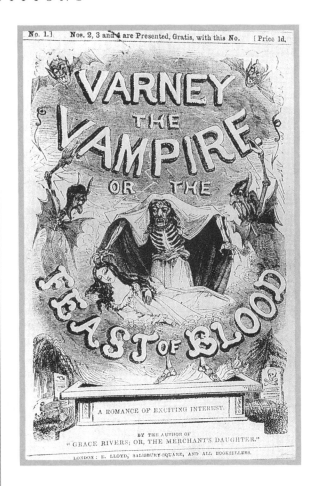

No. 1.]   Nos. 2, 3 and 4 are Presented, Gratis, with this No.   [Price 1d.

VARNEY THE VAMPIRE. OR THE FEAST OF BLOOD

A ROMANCE OF EXCITING INTEREST.

BY THE AUTHOR OF
" GRACE RIVERS; OR, THE MERCHANT'S DAUGHTER."

LONDON: E. LLOYD, SALISBURY-SQUARE, AND ALL BOOKSELLERS.

Superstition

Rheumatism can be cured by wearing a copper bracelet.

Source

Copper was mined from Mother Earth by the people of Bronze-Age and Iron-Age Europe, thousands of years ago. As part of their rituals for removing the natural metals of the earth's deepest core, they would undertake always to be grateful, to give sacrifice and thanks to the earth for allowing this to take place. To remove metals from the earth and use them for making weapons or tools, without proper rituals was considered the worst sacrilege. The believed curing powers of copper derive from this most ancient of sources.

Left: *One of the great superstitions which still retains a powerful emotional charge is that of vampires. This hardy legend has been in circulation for about 450 years. Below: 16th c. French illustrations. Books on the magical and curative powers of herbs and their best cultivation were highly popular during the Middle Ages. Since then they have been of intense interest to country folk and city dweller alike.*

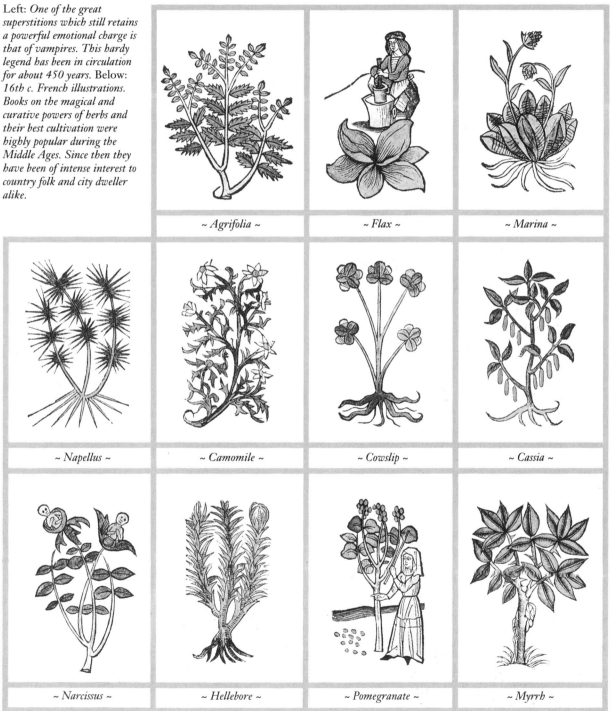

~ Agrifolia ~

~ Flax ~

~ Marina ~

~ Napellus ~

~ Camomile ~

~ Cowslip ~

~ Cassia ~

~ Narcissus ~

~ Hellebore ~

~ Pomegranate ~

~ Myrrh ~

WIVES OR WITCHES?

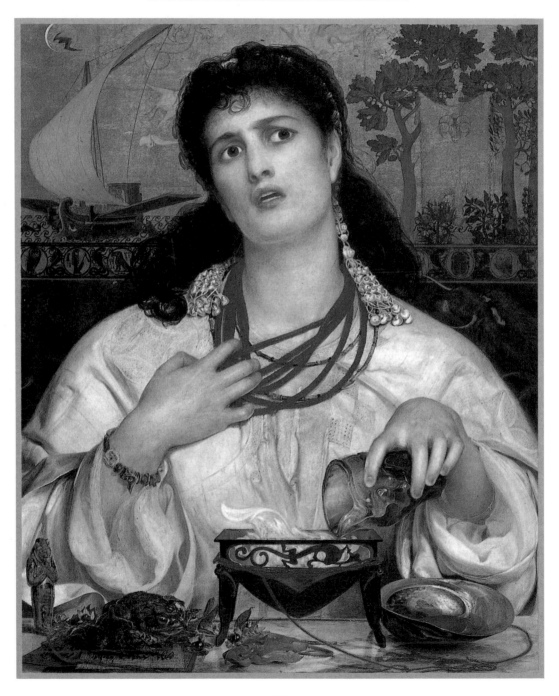

So IF THESE NOTORIOUS OLD WIVES have formulated so many cures and potions, incantations, and herbal remedies, and if they have been doing it for so many hundreds of years, surely there must be some fire beneath the smoke. How successful were they?

A great deal of the herbal knowledge handed down from generation to generation was passed through the female line, from mother to daughter, as part of the domestic understanding. The knowledge was derived from a real understanding of the earth's abilities to cure the bodies it gave birth to. The local wise woman was more familiar with the flora and fauna of the countryside than anyone is today, added to which it was essential for their future success within the community that they were good at their work. The local villages were small, with close-knit, gossiping populations. So an ineffective healer was a hungry healer.

Science today has begun to take a greater interest in the old wives' tale cures and perhaps there is some validity since these remedies have withstood the test of time.

Foxglove, as we have seen in the above section on Cures and Causes, contains the source for the drug digitalis which is currently part of the cures for heart disease. Many other herbal remedies have been found to contain actual curative substances, such as the alkaline content of the dock leaf which counterbalances the acidity of the nettle sting. But more important than all this was the parental nature of the local healer, a security factor in times of uncertainty. The old wife was more like the modern psychoanalyst who spent much time listening to the ailments of her patients and friends and providing numerous methods of keeping people on their feet as opposed to in bed. In China, the equivalent to the shaman or doctor was employed with an additional enhancement to success. He or she continued to be paid while the local population was well. When someone became sick, the pay stopped. One wonders what effect such a method might have on the western medical profession.

The wise woman, whether she is witch or healer, was invariably feared. Her knowledge of the cycles and seasons of life has often been suppressed by dominating male societies, who have managed to distort simple and natural forces into fearful superstitions. Opposite: **Medea**, *by Frederic Sandys. Above:* **Morgan Le Fay** *by the same artist, Birmingham Museum and Art gallery.*

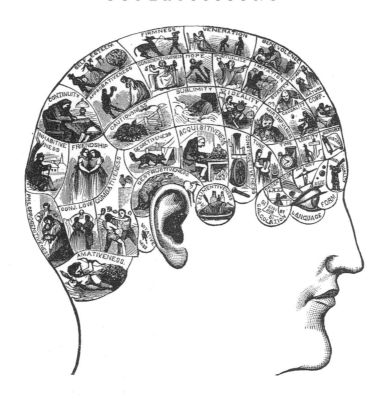

THE BODY APART

MEDICINE IS, OF COURSE, only one application for the mystical and superstitious rituals of the past. There are many wonderful games to be played with the way our bodies look and behave.

One of the favorite comments of visiting relations to any household of children is "Ooh, hasn't he got a high forehead, he must be so intelligent." The "noble brow" theory of high intelligence actually bears no relation necessarily to the truth.

Neither does it necessarily follow that a strong jaw or protruding chin make the proud owner more masculine. The origin of this superstition was that a jutting jaw meant aggression. It's possible to make a whole and not altogether wholesome science out of facial characteristics if we follow this train of thought: close-together-eyes indicate low intelligence; a long pointed, beak-like nose creates a predatory character; thin lips make for meanness and thick for a passionate nature. Human nature and its tendency towards prejudice has frequently used these somewhat arbitrary concepts for less than laudable judgments such as anti-semitic attitudes and problems between races, colors of skin, and creed.

The Victorian English also paid close attention to facial characteristics in their early ideas surrounding psychology and criminology, with very

often disastrous results.

But on a more innocent level, the body offers some delightful opportunities for superstition, such as those centered on the human hand.

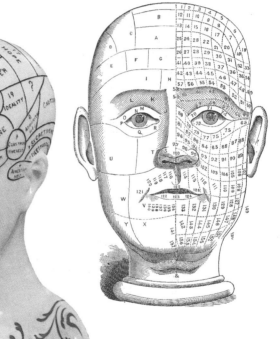

Phrenology, the study of facial lines and bumps on the head was first devised in the late 18th century by Dr. Franz Gall. This quasi-scientific system greatly appealed to the Victorians, much as many of the new age, quasi-mystical systems appeal to our own generation. Shops like the one on the left traded well into this century. While phrenology has not survived the rigours of scientific analysis many of the tenets remained in circulation even now.

HANDED DOWN

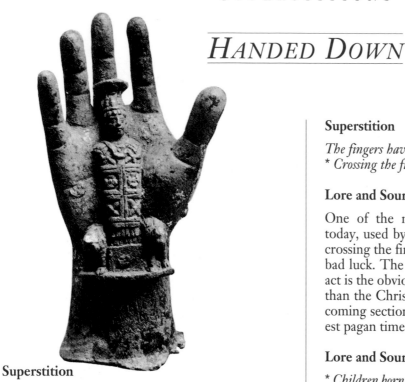

Superstition

That to meet a left-handed man on any day other than Tuesday brings serious bad luck.

Lore and Sources

Some of the very oldest superstitions surround the human hand. The origin of the left-handed man derives from the left-handed Scandinavian god, Tiw, whose name gave rise to Tuesday (Tiw's day). There is still, in some parts of the world, a sinister belief attached to the left side of the body (or anything else for that matter), for in the very earliest pagan times of more than two thousand years ago birds that flew on the left were thought to be unlucky omens. If the left hand acquires an itch, money is forthcoming, and even today at fairs and circuses a visit to a clairvoyant or fortune-teller (originally the village healer or witch) required the crossing of the left palm with silver.

Superstition

The fingers have special powers and particular gifts.
* Crossing the fingers for good luck.

Lore and Sources

One of the most common handy superstitions today, used by all of us at one time or another, is crossing the fingers to counteract the likelihood of bad luck. The symbolism of the holy cross in this act is the obvious source, but the origin is far older than the Christian cross, and as we will see in the coming section on crosses, dates back to the earliest pagan times.

Lore and Sources

* Children born with forefingers longer than second fingers were expected to become thieves.

This was a corollary of the "witch's finger" superstition mentioned earlier, in which the forefinger was used to cast spells or point at unfortunates.

* Still more bizarre are the ideas associated with the white flecks that frequently appear on the fingernails. These can mean either that the bearer is a liar, can foretell the future, or in more modern, medical superstition, has either too much or too little calcium in the body. Conversely, black flecks on the fingernails indicate certain forthcoming death.

Lore and Sources

If we follow superstitious lore, we can get in trouble on almost any day of the week and in particular on the day of rest, Sunday, or the day of infamy, Friday. Clipping the fingernails on either of these days brings bad luck, probably because of associations with working on holy days. The presence of white or black flecks derives from good or bad magic.

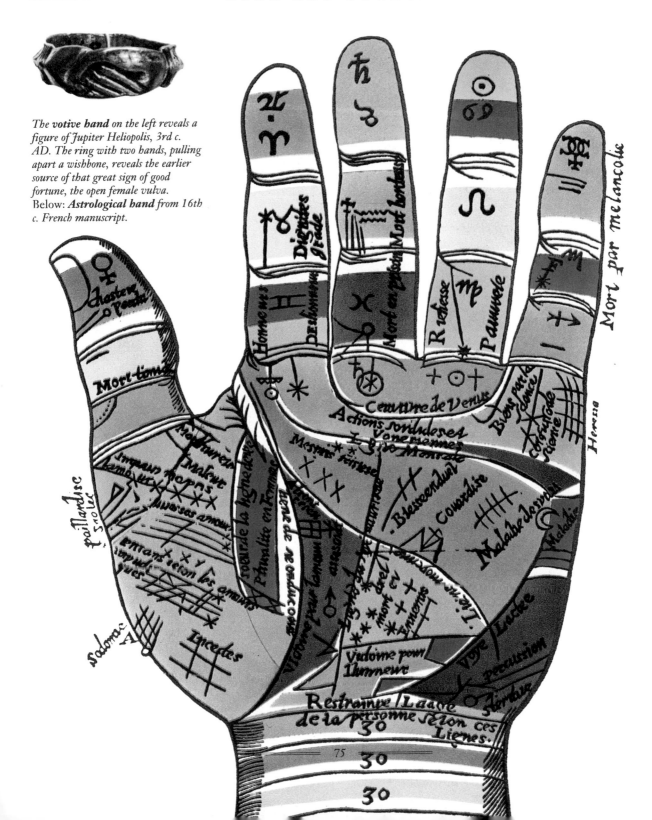

The **votive band** on the left reveals a figure of Jupiter Heliopolis, 3rd c. AD. The ring with two hands, pulling apart a wishbone, reveals the earlier source of that great sign of good fortune, the open female vulva. Below: **Astrological band** from 16th c. French manuscript.

* To shake hands with someone might seem the most friendly of gestures, but should four people shake hands across one another (watch out politicians) they must immediately cross themselves against bad omens or the likelihood of marriage. If they all plan to marry then perhaps the gesture can be employed to good effect. If they do it across a table – well, worse luck for them.

Lore and Sources

To shake hands in the shape of the cross is associated with the danger of sacrilege in imitating the holy cross, so that the friendly gesture indicated by the contact between people is thrown into risk. The table in superstition, represents the coffin, so that to shake hands across a table is to attract death and therefore bad fortune. Many superstitions are connected with placing things, such as umbrellas, shoes or sticks, onto tables, for it was considered a very poor gesture to place anything on the coffin of the dead, for fear of indicating a lack of respect.

* Using the hand for striking a blow gives rise to some gruesome prospects in Scotland.

Lore and Sources

"Your hand'll wag abune the grave for this yet" "abune" meaning above, because of some unfortunate priest who was struck down by a blow and died soon after. His hand was found protruding from above the ground after burial! Yellow spots on the back of the hand portend death also, which puts the average person over the age of forty in dire straits.

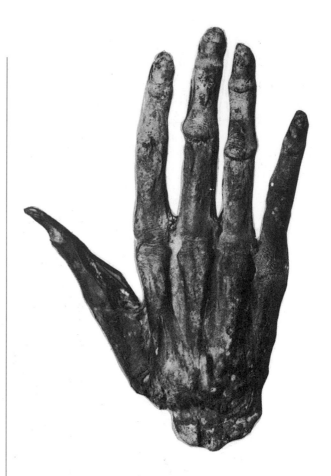

Above: ***Hand of Glory***. *This hand is of a criminal who was hanged in Yorkshire, England. Such grisly relics were supposed to possess very unique powers, especially when they had been treated to become macabre candle holders. For a thief it would open doors, send a household into a drugged sleep and even render the intruder invisible.*

"Let those who rest more deeply sleep, Let those who wake their vigils keep, Oh Hand of Glory shed thy light; Direct us to our spoils tonight."

To be touched by the Hand of Glory could cure migraine, whooping cough and even leprosy.

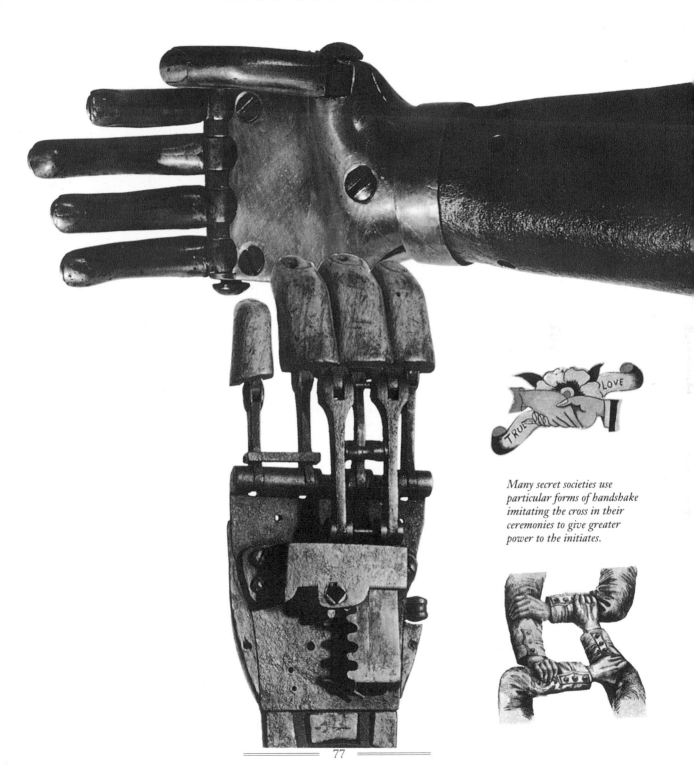

Many secret societies use particular forms of handshake imitating the cross in their ceremonies to give greater power to the initiates.

KEEPING THE HEAD ABOVE WATER

STAYING AFLOAT IN THE FACE of superstition isn't easy, especially when it comes to the various fortunes of the head.

Superstition

A ringing in the ears portends great ill omens if you can't count or recite the alphabet, and quickly.

Lore and Sources

As soon as the ringing occurs you must ask someone else for a number and then count the letters of the alphabet until arriving at the number given. The corresponding letter will then be the first letter of the name of the person one can expect to marry. Ringing in the ears was called "News Bells", and the appropriate letter, once realized could apply also to someone who was either thinking of or talking about the ear-ringer, the presumption being that if someone was thinking about you, he or she would surely eventually wed you. If you should not get the required number instantly then a spinster you would be for ever more! Alternatively, News Bells meant the death of a friend, because the sound of someone's death could be heard at whatever distance.

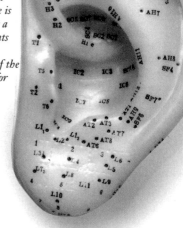

The ear is a part of the head which is hidden and often forgotten, yet it is the single, most sensitive region of the body as far as acupuncture is concerned. There are over a hundred acupuncture points in the ear connected with organs and specific parts of the body which are also used for the new colorpuncture therapies.

Superstition

A common idea even today is that when the ear is burning, others are gossiping.

Lore and Sources

The same reasons applied here – that we can "hear" others speak of us even at inaudible distances. In the original lore the superstition was refined to give a more precise idea of the reason behind the burning ear. "Left for love and right for spite: left or right, good at night." Not satisfied with this, we can of course, hit back at the perpetrator of our condition. "In the case of the right ear I have been advised to pinch it, and the person who is speaking spitefully of me will immediately bite his or her tongue."

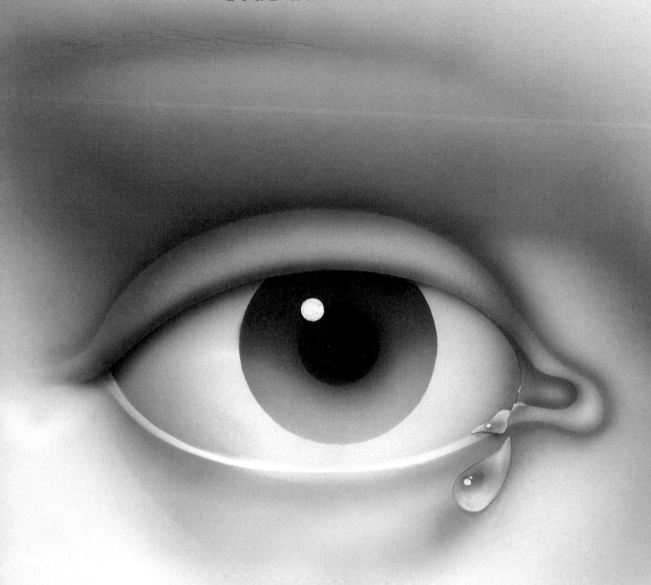

*"If the right eye itcheth, it betokens sorrowful
weeping; if the left . . . joyfull laughter."*
(Homes Daemonologie 1650).

Superstition

If it's the eye that itches we turn, quite naturally, from sound to sight.

Lore and Sources

"My right eye itches now, and shall I see My Love?" (*Theocritus*) And, "Mine eyes do itch: Doth that boade weeping?" (Shakespeare's *Othello*). But the eyes are capable of tears both for mirth and joy: "If the right eye itcheth, it betokens sorrowful weeping; if the left. . . joyfull laughter." (Homes *Daemonologie* 1650).

Superstition

Even the innocent eyelashes came into the story, for losing one meant all manner of dangers.

Lore and Sources

If an eyelash drops out, put it on the back of the hand, make a wish and throw it over the shoulder. If it flies off the hand the wish will be granted. Alternatively it could be placed on the tip of the nose and blown off. The basis for such wishful blowing was once again the devil, who, occupying his normal position behind the left shoulder, presumably made a business of collecting human eyelashes.

During the 18th century the eye became a symbol for the power of reason and was a popular sign representing republican virtues. Here it appears at the top of the pyramid on the American dollar bill.

There was a Young Lady whose eyes,
Were unique as to colour and size;
*   When she opened them wide,*
*   People all turned aside,*
And started away in surprise.

Superstition

Of course, we all know what it means when the eyebrows are hairy and joined together in the middle.

Lore and Sources

"They whose heaire of the eye browes doo touch or meete together, of all other are the woorst. They doo shewe that he or she is a wicked personne, and an intyser of seruauntes, and geuen to unlawfull and naughty artes." Who, after all, would wish to be an "intyser of seruauntes, and geuen to unlawfull and naughty artes?" Women were burned at the stake for no less. There were said to be a great many burnings in Southern Italy and Spain.

Left: *A nonsense limerick by Edward Lear. Perhaps the appeal to solid Victorians of the whimsy of both Lewis Caroll's "Alice in Wonderland" and Edward Lear's "Book of Nonsense" was simply the irrational streak of unreason, so similar to that found in all superstitions.* Above: *Engraving by Gustave Dore for "The Succubus" by Balzac. "Eyes more flaming than I can tell of, from which came a flame from hell". The superstitions of an evil eye remains as potent now as it was a century ago.*

THE FASHIONABLE BODY

THE CLOTHING OF SUPERSTITION is a clear adornment of good or bad fortune. At one time, we all walked around – at least in the warmer parts of the world – stark naked, and clothing was taken onto the body as a form of ritual only. Superstitions once again have grown from such rituals. It was the parts of the body that the clothing covered that endowed them with particular magical qualities which is why the glove has always been of such importance.

Superstition

Casting the glove.

Lore and Sources

The casting down of the glove as a signal of confrontation grew from the original idea that the hand denoted authority and power. Therefore the glove ritualistically took on the qualities of love, greeting, and power. We use this item of clothing somewhat less today, and certainly without much significance, but nevertheless it is of great fascination to look back just a few decades to a time when it featured as the number one ritual adornment in all levels of society.

Picking up ones own dropped glove would bode ill fortune, while to pick up the glove of another was likely to bring a pleasant surprise. The habit of recovering a lady's lost glove, of course, contained strong romantic aspects of gallantry because of the medieval courtly love traditions connected with taking the hand in marriage, a sort of one-step-removed from kissing the woman's hand or the religious ritual of giving the ring in matrimony. The woman must not, incidentally, say "thank-you" when receiving back her glove. Giving gloves as a present is bad luck, and in old Europe the tradition of paying small amounts of money or goods for gifts at weddings was to combat this danger.

The painted and exotic woman as the powerhouse of deception and guile - a perfect source for male fears and superstitions. Above: **Throwing of her Weeds** *by Richard Redgrave, Victoria and Albert Museum Library, London. Opposite page:* **La Belle Dame sans Merci** *by F.G. Cowper, Private Collection, London.*

GETTING KNOTTED

WE HAVE ALREADY, in the beginning of the book, heard something of the perils of untied shoelaces and shoes placed on tables, but knots (including those in shoelaces) have not signified yet in our ever-growing story of potential neuroses.

Superstition

Shoelaces coming undone at the beginning of a new enterprise, dictates shoelace lore, is of the utmost significance – and to a negative effect, while the chance discovery of shoelaces being done up on unworn shoes is good fortune.

Lore and Sources

Knots, among many primitive peoples in the past and still today, are consider to be amulets that protect against evil spirits. This provision was of the greatest importance in preparation for weddings where the sheets of the newlyweds' bed would be carefully knotted prior to the nuptial rituals, and gifts would include knotted handkerchiefs or other garments, each knot being endowed with incantations and spells for good fortune. Equally, a garment that contains an accidental knot may thereby be possessed of demons and bring horrendous consequences to the alliance. It is only a short step from this idea to that of the derogatory English threat, "get knotted," which is used to denote disrespect.

We still use the lucky knot in a handkerchief to remember something. The 19th-century knotted and padlocked Engagement, bracelet, however, has the sinister hallmark of the old chastity belt. The Mexican love-knot, puzzle ring, is of this century.

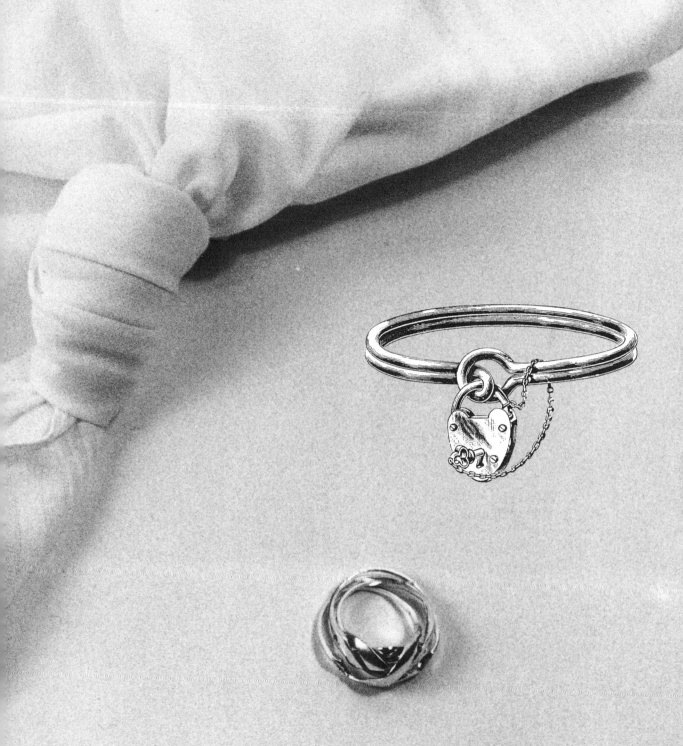

CANNIBAL-RAGS

Superstition

Collecting clothing worn by the famous.

Lore and Sources

The power of human garments has been carried forward from the most gruesome rituals of the past. Today there are ardent collectors of clothing worn by past celebrities. Both the music business and the stage and screen world have given birth to astonishing payments for any garment shed either intentionally or accidentally during concerts or fan "attacks." Entertainers such as Elvis Presley and Marilyn Monroe are the twentieth century inheritors of the rituals initiated by the cannibals of the old world. To eat the body of a tribal chieftain was to acquire his powers, so that to own the clothing of famous stars is to take on whatever qualities are most admired and imagined to have been theirs.

STOCK-IN TRADE

Superstition

Stockings and garters and their powers of good and bad fortune.

Lore and Sources

Stockings, socks, and pantyhose or tights also have their own brand of ritual. One should always put the left one on before the right, and in early times housewives would sew a color stitching into the left one so that the wearer could distinguish between them. If a nylon stocking slips from the garter belt three times in a row there is bad luck afoot, while should your pantyhose on the washing line wrap one leg into the other in the wind in an intimate embrace, joy and happiness will be forthcoming. A run or hole in both legs will ensure a gift, and if you want to receive a vision of your future lover, place your garter belt beneath your pillow at night and you will dream of him. The precursor to the garter belt was the garter which carried considerable romantic power due to its proximity to the genital area.

Superstition

Never wear clothes that have been worn by the dead.

Lore and Sources

The arrangements made for the dead were, since the very earliest times, extremely elaborate and important. The departing soul in ancient Egypt was buried with food, clothes and weapons, to give the best possible chance in the journey across from life into the afterlife. Much of these ancient ideas have survived until today, and to wear the clothes of the dead brings the concept of death closer than is comfortable. It was believed that the clothing would rot with the rotting corpse, and if there were also knots in them, forget good fortune in your life – it would be rotted away forever.

Opposite: ***Garters*** *from a catalogue of S. F. Myers, New York, in 1901. The popularity of such extravagance was far greater in the United States than (with the notable exception below) the more conservative Europe. Below:* ***Can-Can*** *at the Moulin Rouge, Paris.*

Fine Garters.

SOLID GOLD, STERLING SILVER, ROLLED GOLD PLATE AND SILVER PLATED. FITTED WITH FINE ELASTIC SILK WEB IN FANCY COLORS. ALL EXCEPT NOS. 57, 53, 59, 65, 65½, 46, 46½, 47, 47½, 58, 66, 66½ HAVE DETACHABLE PATENT CLASPS. LIST PRICES EACH.

No. 57   Solid Gold, Polished, Chased $26 88
No. 47   Same, Sterling Silver...... .... 6 88

No. 54   Sterling Silver, Turquoise Inlaid.. $6 88

No. 55   Sterling Silver, Satin Bright Cut.......... $6 88

No. 53   Sterling Silver, Satin Polished.............$5 95

No. 56   Sterling Silver, Satin Engraved...........$6 88

No. 59   Rolled Gold Plate, Polished, Engraved.....$4 38

No. 60   Rolled Gold Plate, Roman......   ....$2 45
No. 60½ Same, Silver Plate.......   .... 3 45

No. 61   Rolled Gold Plate, Roman...................$6 88
No. 61½ Same, Silver Plate 6 88

Superstition

Accelerating the delivery of a child can be facilitated by the careful use of a girdle.

Lore and Sources

The delivery of a coming child will be accelerated if the man by whom the woman conceived unties his girdle and, after tying it again around the woman, unties it once more with the incantation, "I have tied it, and will untie it." He then leaves the room for the spell to be effective. The origin of the girdle tied about the mother was the same as the thread winding that was mentioned in the superstition related to curing cramp. Winding something around and around a part of the body was seen to have curative effect, because of its ancient associations with the spinning of thread.

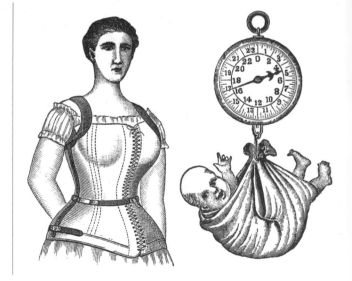

Superstition

The joining of hands in marriage.

Lore and Sources

Remember the wedding ceremony incantation within the Anglican Church which says, "Whom God hath joined together let no man put asunder." Once upon a time a piece of cloth was employed with three knots tied in it, this being placed over the hands of the would-be-weds, and the knot being knitted, the priest would utter, "Whom God hath joined together those let the Devil separate, until these knots be undone."

Brides could, in ancient pagan marriage ceremonies, stand close by the altar with an untied shoe and during the ceremony, the groom would tie the lace to represent the knotting of their marriage.

There are few aspects of life so wrought with superstitious beliefs as that of marriage. This could reflect the importance that this institution once held in the past. Today only a few of these superstitions have survived, yet many of the customs, such as carrying the bride over the threshold are curiously persistent.
Left: ***The Fortuneteller*** *by Caravaggio.* Above: ***The Lovers*** *by Rene Magritte. Richard Zeisler collection New York.*

COLOR-ME-CHAOS

Superstition

The significance attached to the colors of clothing.

Lore and Sources

The color of clothing carries many implications, especially the color green. Whether because of the green of the churchyard or the green of the land, it has long been felt that to wear green is unlucky. Such cheerful recommendations as, "If you wear green your relatives will soon wear black," exist to make us wary of the color, though with the modern determinations of Green awareness, perhaps the evil powers of the color have diminished.

In Victorian times many of the colors dyed into cloth and even wallpapers contained a coloration made with arsenic, particularly the color green, so green wallpaper was considered highly suspect as during the night it might somehow leak the arsenic and poison the sleeper. Green for the Irish, however, denotes precisely the opposite, being the color of the country, it is always associated with good luck there, though it is not the color green itself that is lucky but the people – Irish luck is legendary, and therefore the color green follows suit.

But then you can't really win, because brown is considered equally ill-fated due to its associations with the soil in graveyards and still more so its connection with the brown habits of monks.

With the advent of colortherapy today, we have reverted, behind a quasi-scientific mask, to

the old days. People wearing black clothes are said to be in a process of change, while red indicates that the wearer is going through his or her power trips. There is nothing new that is not old.

In the *Book of Numbers*, dated in the fifth century BC, it was written that young children should always attach a "blue ribband" as a border about the hems of their clothing, and by doing so would find protection from this magic color. It is also said that a certain Lord Burleigh in the seventeenth century, wore blue garters studded with grey snail shells in order to get some relief from his terrible gout!

Blue threads and scarves were worn about the neck during pregnancy to help avoid infections.

The color red probably carries the greatest energy, and at one time, earlier this century, became associated with prostitution and loose sexual morality when worn by a woman. Originally, however, back in the tenth century, red scarves or bands were used either to cure ailments or ward off sickness, and this was the origin of the red scarf worn by bandits over the face, for protection and for disguise.

Above: *Evening dress*, *Gazette du Bon Ton, Sortileges 1922, Victoria and Albert Museum, London*. Opposite page: *The Fitting 1895. Lithograph by Mary Cassatt.*

UMBRELLA – THE SUN-WHEEL

Superstition

Opening an umbrella in the house brings bad luck.

Lore and Sources

Few people today would risk the opening of an umbrella inside the house, but still fewer would know why. The umbrella (umbra in Latin, meaning shade) was originally used by African and Eastern royalty purely as a sunshade. Because of this connection with the sun and also because its shape symbolizes the solar wheel, it became sacrilegious to open it in any shaded area out of the domain of the sun. The superstition was probably greatly reinforced by the fact that the clergy were the first to use umbrellas in burial services long before the general public adopted them for daily use under the rain, though their use by the Church did not have any particular religious purpose – only to protect the good father from the elements.

On the same subject there are other variations, such as never giving an umbrella as a gift or putting one on a table or a bed and dropping one signifies the imminent loss of the mind. There may be some connection here between the umbrella and the sword carried for centuries as a weapon of defense, even in the ordinary streets of a city. Dropping the sword could potentially result in danger to the wearer if there were villains about, and to give a sword as a gift would be an act of aggression.

The parasol or umbrella has been popular throughout the world, but it appears that the superstition concerning the solar wheel is peculiar of Northern peoples. It could be that the sun, being such an infrequent visiting deity, has greater power in the rain crescent of Northwestern Europe.

THE DEVIL'S JEWELS

Superstition

The wearing of jewellry.

And finally, in this chapter of potential and very physical delights and disasters comes the wonder of adornment. How many of us have given serious thought to why we place expensive and beautiful stones and metals about our bodies?

Lore and Sources

Is it simply that we treat ourselves rather like washing lines and attach these things wherever they happen most conveniently to hang, like the ear or the finger, the neck or the arm? Or is there a deeper and more significant reason, like for example the fact that it was always believed that demons could enter the body only through one of the human orifices? It was therefore quite logical to place an earring made of magic materials, suitably empowered with numerous incantations over at least two of them by way of magical defence.

In India it is common to see noserings for the same reason, and protection was afforded to the mouth and eyes by the judicious use of designs and tattoos. To cover the fingers and toes, paint was also employed, and it will not have been lost on the reader that these manifestations of demonic protection have now transformed into the many sophisticated and expensive formulations purchased in drug stores today.

Rings on the fingers were probably the greatest power-containers because of their circular shape, the circle being a symbol of eternity and unity, thus the engagement and wedding rings. A broken ring meant a broken relationship. The engagement ring should always be placed on the third finger of the left hand (the "medical finger"), turned three times while counting to ten, thus guaranteeing good prospects for whoever engineers the act.

It is also commonly believed that stones and metals gain power over periods of time and through various significant experiences such as being worn by magicians or during wars and other important events. Celebrated precious stones carry particular powers, such as the Hope Diamond which is said to bring terrible luck to those who possess it.

This extraordinary diamond was originally known as "The Blue Diamond" and was stolen from the statue of the god Rama Sita in seventeenth century India, later falling into the hands of a Frenchman named Tafernier. The theft was followed by a long series of terrible disasters and the deaths of its owners. Tafernier was eaten alive by wild beasts, while King Louis XIV of France, who received it, died of advanced syphilis, a truly nasty illness. Louis XVI of France, who also owned the diamond, died on the guillotine at the hands of the French revolutionaries.

The diamond eventually came into the hands of Thomas Henry Hope, an English banker, who bequeathed it to his son, who subsequently lost his entire fortune. The stone finally found its resting place with the American diamond merchant Harry Winston who, sensibly, donated it to the Smithsonian Institute in Washington, where it remains today.

The necklace of Marie Antoinette remained unsold at auction during the 1960s because the possession of it is said to cause death to those that come in contact with it, or leave the owner without heirs.

*Elizabeth I. A miniature contributed to Nicholas Hilliard, collection of the Marquis of Salisbury. Above: **The Eugenie diamond**.*

The most active form of stone superstition alive and well during the latter part of this century is crystal magic. In California, London and various other capitals of the world, there are numerous shops and emporiums packed full of every natural crystal that Mother Earth ever spawned, each one attributed with different curative powers and magical qualities. And in astrology there is a firm connection today between physical improvement and various birth stones.

Precious and semi-precious stones are said, in superstitious lore, to carry various qualities and perform various useful tasks. Here are some of the sources of these beliefs.

Amber – *gives health.*

As long ago as the first century A.D., amber jewellry was worn by peasant men and women to protect against witchcraft and disease. The jewel was to be rubbed: "to calefaction (brightness) upon the planetary pulses – the jugular arteries, the handwrists, neer the instep, and on the throne of the heart – and then hung about the neck – becomes the most certaine amulet, to the fatall contagion of this plague."

Amethyst – *protects the owner and prevents narcotic effects.*

The best story relating to the powers of this gentle and delightfully colored stone, is one found in an old tale told in the Middle East around the twelfth century, in which poison drunk from an amethyst cup lost its narcotic effect and left the drinker alive. Worn in a ring, the stone protects against headache, toothache, poison and plague. The amethyst is also mentioned in the Bible (Exodus) as one of the twelve stones that was set in the breastplate of the High Priest, and is also said to have been worn in a ring engraved with a cupid by St. Valentine, the patron saint of lovers.

Coral – *protects babies and lengthens the breaking of the waters in pregnancy. Also signifies friendship.*

Small children were given coral beads or necklaces to be hung about the neck or wrists. This was firmly believed to keep demons from entering the baby's body and protect the child also from witchcraft. Red coral was placed close to the pregnant woman's genitals to prevent the early breaking of the waters before birth, and friendship was assured with a gift of coral because it was thought to be lucky.

Diamond – *cures insanity and tells of incontinence.*

The sources of this superstition are confused and somewhat unlikely, but in any event, people of the fourteenth century in France, according to volume of country folklore published at the time, believed that a diamond held against the forehead of an insane person would cure the ailment, or that if placed beneath the pillow of a wife (evidently not a husband), would betray her incontinence. By the tone of the writing the word "incontinence" may have been wrongly used and the true meaning was intended to be unfaithfulness!

The use of the diamond for insanity may have had some connection with the ancient Buddhist faith where precious stones were often placed at the "third eye" (on the forehead, between the eyes) as an act of religious worship and sacrifice. Diamonds, sapphires and emeralds were also considered to be of great good fortune, both financially, of course, and in terms of their ability to bring luck to the owner.

Elizabeth I. The Rainbow portrait. A miniature attrbuted to Isaac Oliver. In the collection of the Marquis of Salisbury.

NON SINE SOLE
IRIS.

STONE	LORE & SUPERSTITION	STONE	LORE & SUPERSTITION

GARNET *(Wide range of colors)*

Month JANUARY. Associated with strong sexual potency. Warm colors suggest greater passion while green announces a jealous nature.

RUBY *(Red or Red-Blue)*

Month JULY. The wearers of this gem are likely to be passionate and deep lovers. It imparts a high voltage charge to any affair.

AMETHYST *(Purple to Violet)*

Month FEBRUARY. Acts as an antidote to poisons and a protection from disease, plague, headache and toothache. A spiritual stone.

ONYX *(Red and Red-Brown bands with white)*

Month AUGUST. This member of the Agate family reflects a changing nature, as constantly fluid as the patterns it displays.

AQUAMARINE *(Light to Dark Blue)*

Month MARCH. The gem of purification. On a ring it helps composure and a cool head in difficult situations.

SAPPHIRE *(Usually Blue but can be Orange, Pink, Green or Purple)*

Month SEPTEMBER. The great bestower of clarity. Is sure to dispel confusion.

DIAMOND *(Clear, Yellow, Green, Brown or Black)*

Month APRIL. The gem of everlasting ties. Used in magic to strengthen and bind.

OPAL *(Blues and Reds)*

Month OCTOBER. This form of Quartz is a doorway to the Spirit World. It can also signify misfortune and loss of stability.

EMERALD *(Green)*

Month MAY. Traditionally the gem of "far seeing", of divination and prophecy.

TOPAZ *(Ranges from Yellow and Red-Brown to Blue, Green and colorless)*

Month NOVEMBER. This is the gem of Love. It ensures a warmth in any relationship.

PEARL *(White, Cream and Pink)*

Month JUNE. Although popular this organic gem, along with Mother of Pearl signifies tears, sickness and death.

TURQUOISE *(Sky-Blue to Sea-Green)*

Month DECEMBER. Always known as a good luck charm and a protection from evil.

STONE	LORE & SUPERSTITION	STONE	LORE & SUPERSTITION

AMBER (*Yellow, Orange to Red-Brown*)

Health and a protection from Witchcraft.

CITRINE (*Yellow to Orange-Brown*)

Reputed to be unlucky, never the less it is known to assist in creativity.

CORAL (*Black, Pink and White*)

Protects babies and pregnant mothers

SMOKY QUARTZ (*Dark Brown to Smoky Grey*)

Like all the Quartz crystals it is a healing stone. The particular beauty of Smoky Quartz is, however, that it heals evil wounds.

MALACHITE (*Light Emerald Green to Black*)

Releases the power of unknown mysteries and can be used as an evil eye.

TIGER'S EYE (*Warm Brown or Black with silky strata*)

The stone of independence. While it strengthens the wearer it often is said to bring about divorce.

RED JASPER (*Red, Brown and Black*)

This is associated with the body and earthly love. It acts like a magnet and attracts passionate lovers.

AGATE & MOSS AGATE (*Wide variety of banded colors*)

All the Agates share the power of change, whether it is from boredom or from anxiety. Stone of the wanderer.

MOONSTONE (*Transparent with Blue-White sheen*)

The stone of the night which supposedly has power over the Owls and creatures of the night. It protects the wearer from nightmares.

BLOODSTONE (*Mottled Green and Red*)

Once believed to bear the spots of Christ's blood.

ROCK CRYSTAL (*Transparent and clear*)

This purest form of quartz has the power to allow either wearer or practitioner to concentrate. It has great potential to heal.

LAPIS LAZULI (*Intense Blue*)

The stone of Fertility. Also known as the Children's Stone.

Byzantine gold and bejewelled ornament with crucifix. Below: A pearl heart which was very popular as an engagement gift.

Opal – *threaten stability and bring misfortune.*

The opal's variability of color brings it into ill repute within marriage, for marriage, in superstitious terms, need constancy. Queen Maria Cristina of Spain refused to wear a particular opal because it had been owned by a Bourbon family in which no less than five unexplained deaths had occurred. But it seems that the origin of a good or bad luck reputation in a precious stone, can come about simply because of gossip. The source of the opals poor rating evidently derives from the novel *Anne of Gierstein*, by Sir Walter Scott, in which an opal caused the main character to disappear after it was anointed with holy water.

Pearl – *brings tears and indicates sickness or death.*

The ancient Chinese imagined that the pearl was formed within the oyster shell by a drop of rainwater falling from the heavens into the open "bivalves" of the shells and solidifying. The emotional aspect of the human relationship with pearls is based on their similarity with tears, but also because it was noticed that the more this stone was worn, the more varied the colors within it would become. It was supposed that sickness would produce one color and imminent death another.

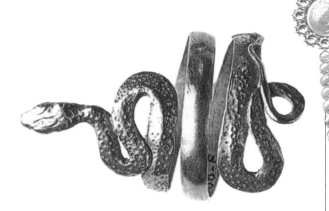

Stones, in fact, have been around as elements of superstition even longer than the stars, for when astrology came into popular existence, the twelve signs of the zodiac already had twelve different stones attributed to them, the same twelve stones that had been given in the Bible to the twelve tribes of Israel.

The stones for each month were: garnet for January, amethyst for February, aquamarine for March, diamond for April, emerald for May, pearl for June, ruby for July, sardonyx for August, sapphire for September, opal for October, topaz for November and turquoise for December.

Above: A 19th-century diamond and pearl ornament of studied opulence with the unlikely name of a 'stomacher'. The prestigious Goldsmiths & Silversmiths Company of London, assured any prospective customer that the jewellery had five matchless 'tear'-shaped pearls", which gives a clue to the emotional significance of the superstition. The vendors coyly refrained from putting a price on this extravaganza but it fetched the modern equivalent of half a million pounds sterling ($900,000).

HYPNOTIC SMELLS

THE MEANING OF THE WORD fascination comes from the original mesmeric powers of the evil eye. The victim was fascinated into a helpless state, and no better substance exists with which to fascinate than perfume. The male was subjected to the ensnarement of the female witch by the use of potions and essences with a strong black magic intention. There was even a time when the use of scents by women was consider potential witchcraft if employed to divert the course of male determination! Still today perfumes are given black magic names such as Tabu and Poison, so that the concept of relationships and the sexual tensions between male and female are still highly charged with the oldest values.

And so, from fascinating fragrances and bedecked bodies, from curious cures and the knitting of knots we move from the temple of the body to the temple of the home and some of the most bizarre and extraordinary lore and sources to cross your threshold of belief.

Left: ***The Perfume Makers*** *by Rudolf Ernst.* Below: *An 18th c.* ***Silver Gilt Flask***, *Musee de Cluny.*

Left: ***The Love Potion*** *by Evelyn De Morgan, Collection of the De Morgan Foundation, London. Below: 17th c. Cloisonne Enamel Flask.*

CHAPTER TWO

THE THRESHOLD OF BELIEF

Men-an-tol *on the South West coast of Cornwall, England. This mysterious megalithic structure is believed to possess powerful healing properties. The image of the twin stones with the holed one in between suggests a structure used in initiatory rites of passage. Passing through the stone would appear an obvious symbol for both passing through the birth canal from the womb into this world or of moving out of this world and into another, either in death or initiation.*

The threshold from one reality to another is a powerful theme in any belief system or superstition.

HEARTH AND HOME

IT IS NOT ALTOGETHER A COINCIDENCE that the words "hearth" and "heart" are so similar. In the last chapter we delved into the ways in which humanity has surrounded the body with an extraordinary number of mystical and magical protections, against demons and devils, poison and passion, basically with always the same motivation, to counter the unknown. The heart was deliberately left out of the physical story because in the most direct ways it takes its place in our ever-growing tale of superstitious belief as a connector between the body and the home.

The hearth is the place where the fire is built to warm the "cockles" of the heart. Keeping "the home fires burning" was a fundamental need during wartime England and symbolized mankind's desire to cherish family and friends, love and security. This has always been the case. We use the word heart in so many contexts which connect our mystical beliefs to daily life that it quickly becomes evident what an important organ it is, above and beyond that continuously pumping machine whose job it is to circulate the life-blood throughout our bodies.

We "take heart" in a situation that requires confidence. We love our closest friends and relatives "with all our hearts," and we have "heart-to-heart" talks in order to express our inner-most feelings. We can sometimes be "heartless" when we are afraid or angry, and we "lose our hearts" to others or "find our hearts in the right place" when we need to be generous. We become "sick at heart" or "hearty", "heart-broken," and "full of heart" in different situations, all of which are connected with love and concern in everyday life.

If we think of the body as a kind of temple in which we exist and live through our lives, the skin is the body's outer layer of protection. Beyond the skin, then, the next layer of protection in which we live is the home. The body and the home, therefore, are connected in all manner of ways, not only between the heart and the hearth. We have formulated literally hundreds of phrases that make this contact possible, perhaps because we doubt it. There is always a sense within humanity that we are somehow separated from the

Far left: *A Peep into Futurity*. *A 19th c. engraving by D. Maclise. A young woman gazes into the fire while interpreting the cards. Her cat familiar sits with an inscrutable stare into the warmth of the hearth.* Right: *The heart or hearth is central to all superstitions. To strike at the heart of things is a saying well known even today. This is a bottle which contained a cloth heart stuck through with pins which was found earlier this century. What happened to the target of this malicious attack is unknown.*

world by our egos, doubts, and fears, so that it is constantly necessary to reaffirm the connection using words and ideas.

We talk about the "rib cage" as though our chest cavity were imprisoned by the bones that surround it. We "swallow our pride" as though the outside world had given us a nasty medicine. We "let off steam" as though we were a kettle being boiled by existence, and we "re-charge our batteries" like cars after a heavy traffic jam.

When we come closer to magic and superstition it becomes clear that not only do we depend entirely on our homes and friends for our continued survival but that the hearth is as much part of the human body as the heart and lungs that lie within it.

THE PSYCHIC CENTER & THE SACRED THRESHOLD

IF WE CONTINUE THIS MOVEMENT away from the body and imagine the home in which we live as a direct extension of us and our heart-thumping lives, we can soon begin to appreciate that the heart beats throughout our houses and even into our neighbor's next-door retreat.

Traditionally, in exactly the same way as the skin protects the body, so the doors, windows, and roof of our house protect us from the intrusions of unwanted people and the invasion of the elements. In cities today we might have three or four locks on the door and a video-electronic entry-phone that allows us to appear to be "out" if an unwanted caller rings our bell. Many people leave their answering machines on permanently and pick up the receiver only when a welcome voice begins a message. We employ electronic alarm systems, lock our valuables up in "safes," and take out expensive insurance policies to repay us from the unwelcome visit of a burglar. We even, in some parts of the world, fear for our lives from within our homes. The phrase "there's no place like home" begins to show its wear and tear in modern society. All the more need, therefore, for the employment of every conceivable form of magic that might offer itself!

Superstitions that surround the house are among the most ancient of all, that is, if we define a house to include even the most primitive dwellings. In times that might now be regarded as immeasurably old, it was believed that spirits commanded all activities within the home. Although we have largely lost this protection because we now regard the solidity of science as more reliable, there are still some vestiges of the spirit of the home remaining. When we enter a new home that we hope to buy, we often make a judgment based on a "welcoming" factor. Does the place feel good or bad to us? In ancient times this atmosphere would have been dictated by very definable concepts such as the presence or lack of gods and goddesses, spirits, and demons within each and every part of the house.

When we walk into a house for the first time or enter the house of another person with whom we are not familiar, we invariably do so through the front door, not the back door. Many front doors, especially in Europe, have carved sprites such as cherubs above the center of the door, and there is still the common habit of hanging either a horseshoe or a flower garland on the door itself. These would once have been important symbols of protection against the entry of evil spirits

into the house. The horseshoe must be hung with the "legs" up so that the luck cannot run out of the shoe.

So let us now take a closer look at some of the most fascinating superstitions related to the home, and the sources from where they were originally born.

Left: The image of the Celtic goddess, Sheela-na-gig. There are examples of her likeness appearing at the threshold of churches for she is, herself, thought to be a threshold to the magical otherworld.
Upper left: **Magical Well**, *Cornwall, England. Even today the custom of hanging 'lucky cloth still persists.* Above: **Chun Quoit**, *Cornwall. A Stone doorway to   an ancient burial mound.*

It is hardly surprising that this huge phallic menhir in Brittany has a Gaelic reputation for being a powerhouse of fertility. Barren wives and newly weds must visit the site at midnight to ensure a pregnancy. To sleep with the menhir all night is a guarantee of seven children.

Superstition

The Petting Stone.

There are two stories that started this superstition, one from ancient Rome and one still older. The bride had to be carried over the threshold for fear that if she was not she was in danger of losing her virginity to the earth rather than to the new husband. In parts of Scotland at the beginning of this century brides were still carried over the first step of the house for fear that some witchcraft would be carried by her into the home. The groom, of course, was free both of the risks involved in virginity and the chances of witchcraft!

The second, and still more fascinating source of this superstition also brings a word into the modern love vocabulary, that of "petting."

At Lindisfarne Abbey on Holy Island in Northumberland, England, the ancient King Ethelwold "caused a ponderous Cross of stone" called a "socket-stone" to be erected in the ground of the Abbey. It later became known as the "Petting Stone," and on all occasions of marriage ceremony the bride had to step upon the stone. If she was unable to stretch her stride to the end of it, then the marriage would prove unhappy. The stone was said to be the pedestal of St. Cuthbert's Cross, and therefore carried great mystical power, though why it was named the petting stone is not now known.

In various other parts of England there are still petting stones where the bride is expected either to stretch her legs across them or be carried over them in order to satisfy the superstitious beliefs. The love-play between couples prior to lovemaking derives its name from this source.

And to return us to our train of thought, the visitor to a house, who has stepped over the threshold, must exit by the same door and should he or she have reason to return unexpectedly, thus breaking the direction of the journey to go back to the house again, it is necessary to sit down in the road and count from the number seven backwards before resuming the trip. The departing guest must also not be watched out of sight as if he is, he may never return. The

sources behind this complex superstition range across much of the ancient lores handed down to us. Exiting through the same entrance as had been taken into the house was thought to complete the visit correctly, for thresholds existed both at the front and the back of the house and a visitor should not cross them both, but only re-cross one. Turning around after leaving the house and directly returning over the threshold was thought to be unlucky for similar reasons. The visitor should "take a breath" before making a new visit. The gods demanded it, the earth "gave sanctity to it." Counting backwards confused the devil and the number seven was a magical number that gave power to the end of one journey and the beginning of another. All very complicated, but all very necessary!

Lores and Sources

The sacred threshold carries a magic of its own, rather like the barrier between the outside world and the inside intimacy of the home, in the same way as the skin acts for the body. We don't let just anyone enter over the threshold. We relax behind the threshold in ways that we never can beyond it, and the people that we welcome into our homes must pass certain important qualifications before they can step over that barrier. The most extreme form of this is carrying the bride over the threshold after marriage. In the light of the feminist developments of the last decades this concept has died a violent death. We might imagine that originally it arose from the patriarchal and property delineations that most of mankind lived by. The male line inherited the property and the female was accepted into it, but the truth is far more interesting.

Above: *One of the **Altarnum circle of stones** on Bodmin moor in South West England. Not only are these stones supposed to be charged with vital energies which affect both men and women, they also appear to attract cattle. Photo by Mick Sharp.*

Superstition

Houses should not be given the number thirteen.

Lore and Sources

From the most ancient times, the number thirteen was ill-fated, primarily because of the violent deaths of various ancient thirteenth gods, and of course the fate of the thirteenth guest at Jesus' Last Supper. Why is it that in many skyrise office and apartment buildings, the thirteenth floor does not exist, at least not on the elevator panel?

Below: ***The Last Supper*** *by Leonardo da Vinci. The number 13 was considered unlucky because there were thirteen at Christ's last supper. In fact the bad luck connected with the number preceded the Christian legend.*

The Last Supper *by Salvador Dali. The lengths to which some hotel managers cater to superstitious guests can be observed at the Carlton Hotel in London. It is described as having 18 floors but in actuality there are only 17 as the number 13 is missing.*

Even royalty is not immune to such beliefs. When Princess Margaret, the sister of the present Queen of England, was born in Glamis castle, the registration of her birth was delayed so that her number in the register would not be the unlucky 13.

THE HEARTH OF THE MATTER

Superstition

The magic surrounding the open hearth and its fire.

Lore and Sources

We began this chapter by linking, phonetically, the words heart and hearth, but the connection goes far deeper. The hearth or open fire was a focal point of the household because it contained the most ancient of all elements, fire itself. The sacred flame of the gods discovered by earliest man has been carried by the tribes of humanity for tens of thousands of years. The tribes would appoint a single individual whose sole responsibility was to keep the flame going at all times as a symbol of life, and quite simply a very practical necessity.

For the Romans, the homely spirit Penate guarded the hearth, and later in medieval dwellings Hob was the house-fairy that protected the hearth from demons, thus the use in England of the word hob in kitchens.

A visitor to another home may never poke the owner's fire until he has been a friend for seven years because it takes that long for friendships to mature, and no stranger may insult the Hob fairy. Why seven years? Because the body undergoes a complete physiological change every seven years and thus the friendship cannot be integrated physically in less time. Thus we protect our homes from strangers.

Lighting a fire is also beset by numerous ground rules. A fire which will not light is in danger of attracting evil spirits because of the ancient beliefs surrounding the perpetuation of fire, so that it is necessary to take the poker and place it in the shape of a cross over the front bars of the fire. And a fire cannot be lit successfully if there is a ray of sunlight shining directly on the hearth. This comes from the very beginning of time itself as the original belief was that fire was stolen from the sun, and if the sun shines on a hearth it looks in derision at the pathetic attempts to ape its power.

We may say that all this is evidence of our fear, and ineptitude simply makes us prisoners of the past, but seen from the light of the sun it also carries a tremendous mystical value once brought into the cockles of our hearts.

Below: ***The Tournament*** *from "In Fairyland" by Richard Doyle 1870.*
Opposite page: ***The Fairy Feller's Master Stroke*** *by Richard Dadd, Tate Gallery, London.*

REFLECTIONS OF FEAR

GETTING INTO THE HOME without incurring the wrath of one of the many gods is difficult enough, but once inside there are a plethora of impending traps that must carefully be observed. The item that most readily presents twentieth century man with pangs of uncertainty is the mirror.

Superstition

Breaking a mirror brings bad luck for seven years.

Lore and Sources

The superstitions surrounding the mirror are some of the oldest, for they relate to the idea that our reflection is another version of the original, and if we somehow manage to damage the mirror we are therefore damaging ourselves, damaging the reflection is damaging the soul. Vampiric legend reflects most closely the negative aspect of mirror superstition, for, as we commonly understand, a vampire has no soul and therefore no reflection, and as the blood of the victim is slowly drained from the body and the vampire's incisors make their mark, so the individual watches his reflection in the mirror slowly disappear. Even a disturbance in the reflection can cause an imbalance in the relationship between body and soul, and this is where the seven years of bad luck comes into the story. As always the period of bad luck is seven years because of the belief that the body changes its physiological make-up every seven years.

If we manage to break a mirror, however, as with all the best superstitions, there are remedies that will reverse the fortune of the damaged soul. We can take the broken pieces of the mirror and wash them in a south-running river, thus washing away the bad luck. Or we can bury them in the earth and thus neutralize the potential evil. Taking the mirror's remains out of the house is an essential move and to look into a cracked mirror is ill-advised. Any reflecting surface that is broken can be as dangerous as a mirror, and it is said that even the inside of a thermos that has broken should be washed at once.

The original source for washing the broken mirror lies far in our past. In the book of Psalms, written 200 years before Christ, come the words: "I will wash my hands in innocency: so will I compass thine altar, O Lord." In numerous other tracts and documents, both in Europe and early America, washing the hands and body in relation to holy acts and processes of holy ritual is commonly related. The concept of washing was something largely connected with religion. In fact, to wash at any other time was considered a bad idea, for it would wash away the soul unless there was some sanctity attached to the act.

We take washing so much for granted today, that our hygiene has outweighed our sense of the holiness of washing. Only baptism remains as a residue of one of the oldest superstitious and holy acts.

Those that have spent time in the home of grandparents that were born at the beginning of this century may be aware of the superstition that states we must cover a mirror except when in use because it attracts lightning. In the homes of the recent dead, a mirror must remain covered or the departing soul may take the soul of a living relative along on the journey for company. Alternatively, it is said that a mirror should be covered in the house of the dead because death ends vanity.

*Opposite: **The Baleful Head** by Edward Burne-Jones, Staatsgalerie, Stuttgart. Here Perseus is showing Andromeda the head of Medusa reflected in a mirror-like pool. The reflected image has many connotations in folk tales. The Vampire has no image while some creatures or fears can only be viewed indirectly. Some folk beliefs maintain that you can only see the spirits of the departed in a mirror and of course the fortune teller's crystal ball is yet another mirror-like surface. Above:* **Mirror of Venus** *by Burne-Jones, 1878, Gulbenkian Foundation, Lisbon.*

Above: *The extraordinary world behind the mirror as envisaged by Lewis Carroll and drawn by John Tenniel.* **From Alice's Adventures Through the Looking Glass***.*

Opposite page: **Not to be Reproduced** *by Rene Magritte, 1937, Museum Boymans-van Bevningen.*

We can go still deeper into the mythology of the looking glass because it was a common tool of magicians, wizards, and witches in ages that are long gone into the darkness of the past. Should the breakage occur at the paws of a cat, the story gets worse, and worse mainly because cats were the familiars of these dangerous professionals.

The doubts and digressions of the world of magical reflection also leak over into pictures on the wall, or rather off the wall, on the basis that anything which is supposed to be in its place in the home, which breaks the rule and falls to the floor, is bad luck. But there are differences in the degree of bad fortune according to what is in the picture. If it is a portrait of someone in the house and it falls or becomes tilted on the wall, the superstition derives from the same source as those connected to mirrors. But whereas a mirror is only a reflection of the original person, a picture, in magical terms, is as good as the original and therefore constitutes greater bad luck. The result is the likely death of the person in the picture.

WOODWAYS TO THE GODS

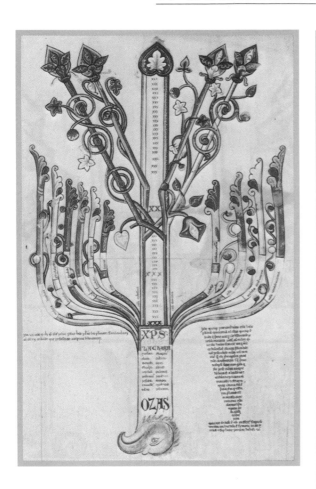

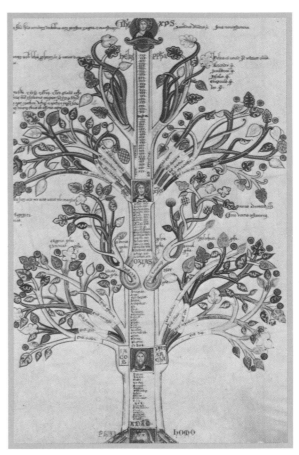

*Trees and the particular patterns and forms of living wood, have always made rich metaphors for concepts like these 14th c. **Trees of History**, Sennario Vescoville, Reggio Emilia.*

Superstition

Stairs, bannisters, ladders and touching wood.

Lore and Sources

Stairways and ladders remain powerful reference points in our continued superstitious attitudes. Never pass someone else on the stairs and never walk under a ladder, but why? Simple enough.

The stairs in a house are the means by which we reach the gods, as in Jacob's Ladder in the Bible. But there is hope for where there is transgression, so also there is solution. Christ is always, in Christian superstitious belief, the most powerful of the gods so that in transgression we can always make the sign of the cross, and Christ will come to our aid against the lesser mighty.

Banisters are almost invariably made from

wood, stretching from the top of the stairs to the ground at the bottom. Wood might seem a sensible material for such use, but there were also other reasons for the choice originally.

The ancient Celtic peoples of Europe, who formed perhaps the single most powerful "tribe" of

Western mankind for many centuries before Christianity, worshipped the tree as the foremost earthly representation of the gods. If bad fortune visited in the form of demons or devils, or if a battle was about to be fought, the power of a tree was invariably brought into force. The Druidic priest performed all of his rituals and incantations within the sacred arbors that stood in place of the modern church or the ancient stone circle. There are those also that would assert that the superstitions surrounding wood also derive from the material from which the cross of Jesus was made.

As a natural result of these origins we touch wood today, for wood takes the evil spirit and quickly sends it plummeting to earth. Even before the Celts, though, the ritual of touching earthly elements was alive with the Iron Age peoples who mined Mother Earth for her natural materials and

Illustrations from the Illustrated London News 1851/1880 showing that hanging mistletoe at Christmas was a popular Victorian custom. It preceded the later custom of the Christmas tree which was introduced by Queen Victoria's Consort, Prince Albert

smelted iron with only the most complex rituals, for they feared that the diurnal gods would punish man for stealing the possessions of the deepest underground. So, touch wood or touch iron for safety.

So, as we pass by the dreaded gods on our way up the stairs to the danger zones of darkness, keep the hand firmly placed upon the wooden banister, and all evil demons will be consumed in the ground.

BED NOBS AND BROOMSTICKS

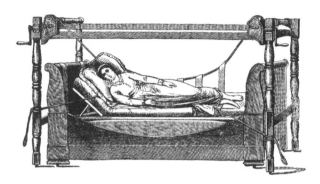

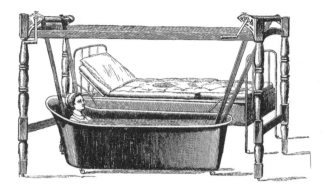

AND ONCE UPSTAIRS and ready for sleep, we must beware to observe the conditions surrounding the bed that will contain us in the dangers of the night.

Superstition

The bed must be positioned in the room according to strict rules.

Lore and Sources

We have heard already in the first chapter of the necessity of making sure that the position of the bed is exactly in line with the direction of the floorboards and never across them, but did we know also that the head and feet must lie in a north-south direction in alignment with the magnetic pole? There are others who will demand that blocks of wood or other items be placed under the bottom legs of the bed so that the head is at a lower position than the feet, due to the assertion that it is healthier for the body to sleep this way.

Right: *Detail of an engraving by William Hogarth, dated 1762 (see page 24). It shows a witch riding her broomstick while suckling her cat from her third nipple.* Above: **Duponts Multiple Apparatus 1850.**

Superstition

Getting up the right way in the morning.

Lore and Sources

Getting up in the morning is, of course, still more important than going to bed, for example, making sure that each item of clothing is put on without dropping to the ground. And getting out of the bed on the right side (as opposed to the wrong or left side) is vital for the coming day, though who decides which is right and which is wrong is hard to discover when examining the ancient lores. The only real source concerned with what is the right and what the wrong side of the bed comes, once again from the fisherman's world. No sensible fisherman during the nineteenth century would ever board his boat on the left side, however inconvenient it might be.

It seems that this superstition originally arose out of the idea that anything left-handed was unnatural, on the basis that the majority of human beings were right-handed! Left feet were unlucky, as were left hands, so that getting out of bed on the left side had also to be unlucky.

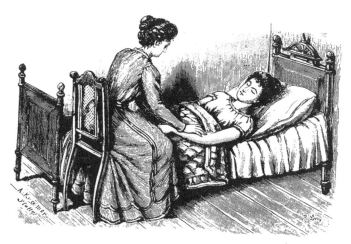

Superstition

Bed-making must be performed according to certain rules.

Lore and Sources

When making the bed before leaving, don't interrupt your work until it is completed or you will spend a restless night in it, and avoid sneezing while making the bed or the soul rushes out of the body and into the bed, bringing poor sleep again that night. Never turn a mattress on a Sunday or death will soon result in that bed, and if you start making a bedspread, be sure to finish it or marriage will not come to you or your home.

Superstition

Brooms, cleaning and their requirements.

Lore and Sources

And now that the night has been passed, the bed made, and the bedspread finished, you can begin cleaning the house before leaving for work. Just be sure not to buy or make the broom (besom) in May, the Roman month of death. "Brooms bought in May sweep the family away."

In England, one of the most common door-to-door salespeople was the brush-seller, and in May, unlike most other business people, the brush-seller would take an annual vacation.

And most popular of all superstitions is probably the one that says the witch flew about on a broomstick. It's not true, of course, but just in case before leaving for work place the broomstick in front of the door and she will pass along the street to another house, thinking that your house already has its own resident witch.

SALT-SELLERS AND OLD SALTS

SOON ENOUGH IN OUR THRESHOLD mysteries we come to the diet. Food occupies a vast area of interest for the uncertain of heart and new superstitions are being born every year with every new diet that is published! But if we go back into the more distant past we find most readily the presence of the purest substance on earth as the beginning and the end of ritual insecurity. For salt was the one absolute pure substance as well as being the most common preservative, and no medieval home was without several bags of it.

In Italy there are still signs outside thousands of small bars and shops scattered across the country which read – "Sale e Tabacci" – "Salt and Tobacco." These "salt-sellers" don't, of course, sell only salt and tobacco and probably never did restrict their trade so severely. The reason why the signs are there, more than a hundred years old in most cases is because both salt and tobacco were at one time monopolized by the Italian government. You could not buy them anywhere other than licensed outlets. In the same way as governments today with regard to tobacco and alcohol, Italy made an income from salt and tobacco, though not alcohol. But why salt? In fact, why is salt so important a substance in many areas of life – especially in matters of superstition and magic?

Salt came (and still does) from Mother Earth, from the sea. The tears and the saliva tasted of salt. Man's most readily available food came from the sea, and his world was more ocean than land. The cooperation between man's eating habits and the sea was bridged by salt, was flavored by salt.

Silver and Gilt Salt, 16th c. Jewel House in the Tower of London. This salt shaker was used at coronation banquets up until the early part of this century. In mediaeval times to be "below the salt" meant that the salt containers did not go beyond a certain point on the table. Thus those beyond that invisible social line had to put up with none.

"With all thine offerings thou shalt offer salt." (*Leviticus* 585 B.C.) In Homer's *Iliad* Patroclus scatters the embers and lays the spits above them after sprinkling the meat with holy salt for sacrifice to the gods. Probably the use of salt as a condiment and embellishment for food arose simply from this ritual. It helped to appease the gods and it tasted good too!

Superstition

Spilling salt is unlucky.

Lore and Sources

All the way from ancient Greece until today, the spilling of salt is the most unlucky of accidents unless you quickly take a pinch and cast it over the left shoulder "right into the Devil's face." For the devil dances at our left (sinister, unlucky) side just waiting for our sinful natures to give up our souls forever. Salt will temporarily blind "Old Nick" (the devil) until the soul can once again be secured by good fortune.

At the table never pass the salt directly to another, but set it down so that the guest may pick it up again, and take salt to a new house, bringing good fortune with it.

Superstition

Scattering fishermen with salt for good fortune at sea.

Lore and Sources

Women left at home by their seagoing husbands would go to the rocks beside the sea's edge and

Home Again, a detail of painting by A. Grimshaw. The wealth of intricate
customs and superstitions surrounding the sailor, his woman and the sea, was of
course most noticeable during the great days of sail around the turn of the 19th
century. Yet even now if a departing sailor tastes the salt of his beloved's tears, he
knows he will return safety and his lover or wife will be faithful.

pour handfuls of salt into the cracks, in this
way helping to bring their spouses back from
the dangers of the oceans. Fishermen leaving for
a day's haul would be showered with a little salt
for good luck. The most ancient sources of
superstitious rituals such as these lie in the lores of
the land, where men and women acted in cooperation and respect for the substances of the ocean and
the land in the hope that the feeling would be
reciprocated.

TEA-TIME

IN ENGLAND DURING THE POST-WAR YEARS there were advertisements in trains and buses that read: "Eat bread, the staple diet." As children, did we ever question what a staple diet was? Somehow bread was simply essential. In the small villages of 1950s England, bakeries produced all the bread for the local area, and the smell of the baking pervaded the entire area every early morning. Mothers and grandmothers everywhere would take a loaf every day, tuck it under the arm, butter it first and then slice the thinnest slices, that melted in the mouth!

But then, one terrible day, there came something which in England was called "Sunblest" bread, wrapped in plastic and already sliced, tasting of plastic, and putting the local baker out of business.

Bread superstitions today are, as a result of this modern technological innovation, largely extinct.

Superstition

Never waste bread.

Lore and Sources

Originally to waste bread was regarded as sacrilege, "If you throw away bread you will follow the crow for it." Every last crumb of the daily loaf was to be consumed before any fresh bread could be baked, and the girl who ate the last slice would be blessed with either marriage, "ten thousand a year" (the currency is not mentioned) or both. The derivation of this custom is found in the oldest cornfield rites when the last sheaf of wheat or corn was plaited into a "kern baby" and given to an unmarried girl who would then be blessed with marriage and money that season. All this, of course, takes us back into the original earth-rites that sustained the local community by attaching it securely to the harvest and the seasonal blessings of the ground. Thus the English tradition of afternoon tea-time with its sandwiches and tea.

Superstition

Holy bread is the body of Christ.

Lore and Sources

The holy bread of the Church is still blessed out of reverence to an extremely ancient tradition, sourced long before Jesus Christ sat with his disciples at the Last Supper. Even though today and for the last sixteen hundred years it has been directed towards "the body of Christ," this was really only the Christian version of the original design and another example of how the Church incorporated the oldest rites into its own beliefs.

Bread and indeed all manner of other foods were considered the body of the earth, received from the ground and accepted as sustenance with the correct rituals.

Bread was kept under the heads of children when sleeping and a crust could be carried in the pocket against "hags" and other dangerous black magicians. A piece of bread would be wrapped into a baby's bib or clothes to protect the child from any witchcraft or evil demons. It was also considered bad luck to cut bread rather than break it, though if the cutting was done with a skewer in the form of a cross over the top of the loaf, then this was acceptable. Here, presumably, comes the derivation that has resulted in "hot-cross-buns" which were originally only baked on Good Friday before Easter.

The English Hot-Cross-Bun is just one of a variety of sacred breads. Many are only baked on a Holy day like Good Friday. A Hot-cross-bun left under a baby's pillow will keep the devil at bay and ensure a good night's sleep for everyone.

Superstition

The rites and rituals of drinking tea.

Lore and Sources

It has long been a mystery to people of most nations why the English are so fond of tea. This extraordinary brew will be consumed at almost any time of the day or night, with breakfast, at "elevenses," for lunch, at teatime, before dinner and last thing at night. The English drink it from mugs, cups, and even out of the saucer to cool the concoction. Even today tea has retained a large part of its ritual nature and we may apply the old stories to it with equanimity.

Never stir the tea in the pot "widdershins," that is from right to left, for this will forebode a quarrel, and if two women pour their brew from the same pot, one of them will become pregnant within a year. This apparently has something to do with phallic symbolism of the spout. Thou shalt not put the milk into the tea before the sugar for fear of crossing love by so doing, and to put the boiling water into a teapot before the tea will bring bad fortune.

Even today, tea-leaf reading is common at carnivals and fairs, and many a future fate is gleaned from the ritual throwing of the leaves

across the inside of a cup. The process requires the reader to drink the tea first, until one teaspoon of tea remains, then hold the cup in the left hand and move it three times in a circular, counter-clockwise direction, then slowly pour the liquid contents into the saucer, thus leaving the leaves in the bottom and sides of the cup. Looking into the cup you will see various shapes and images in the pattern of the leaves, and these are the basis for the reading. Leaves in the shape of a heart mean future happiness, dots indicate money, two hearts mean marriage.

19th-century engraving of an old gypsy telling a young girl her fortune in the leaves. According to the mediums, the shapes created by the leaves relax the fortune teller's mind, allowing free associations to take substance while, at the same time, picking up feelings from the client

THE POWER OF THE FLOWER

Superstition

The giving of different flowers and their significance.

Lore and Sources

Flowers are still among the most popular of ritual gifts, and unlike other produce cannot yet easily have their essence destroyed by technology and science. A rose is ever a rose, for not even science can retain the smell, touch, look, and magic once the petals are plucked for closer examination.

All the way from ancient Egypt and the pagan followers of Mother Earth, a gift of flowers brought good fortune and love so that the massive industry all around the world that grows and distributes the numerous varieties has done nothing but disperse good luck to us all.

Marigolds may be safely brought into the home for they are the flowers of the sun, while the daffodil, Wordsworth's favorite, was once used as a substitute for sacrifice and should therefore be adored only outside. Roses are a symbol of love and must therefore be given to the bride on her wedding day, while any purple flower brings good fortune in finance. The white carnation, often worn by the bridegroom and the ushers at a wedding ceremony, means an offering of pure love (as opposed to sexual love) and admiration, and Mimosa, white lilac and heavily scented flowers of any kind are to be employed at funerals and therefore tend to indicate bad fortune. Red and white flowers together must not be brought into the home because of their ancient association with diseased lovers from Roman times.

Once again, much of the more poetic and dramatic aspects of flower superstition derive from the pagan sacrifice rituals of thousands of years ago. The May hawthorn flower was braided and used to crown the heads of those to be sacrificed to the harvest, and many flowers, such as the snowdrop, were thought to contain the souls of the dead within their petals.

In the more remote parts of England, there is still undertaken the beautiful ritual of flower pairing, in which sets of two flowerbuds are taken to a secret location such as a hayloft. Here the names of all the young lovers in the local village are written onto pieces of paper and tied about the stamens of the flowers, each flower being cut to indicate the height of each young person. The flowers are then left to blossom, and as they grow and change their position, some will entwine themselves around each other. Each "couple" created indicates the romantic potentials in the village. If a flower turns away from another then an estrangement is indicated, and blossoming early shows a likely offspring. A flower that dies early will forebode the death of the individual, and a downcast position indicates sickness.

*During the 19th-century the language of flowers reached an extraordinary degree of complexity. Each flower had its own inner meaning to the aficionado. Anemones meant withered hopes. A Lily was thought to be unlucky and fickle. Carnations meant marriage and eternal love and remain today the most popular flower at weddings. Forget-me-nots were sent to tell of true love. A skilled arranger could, with this floral vocabulary, actually send a clear and precise message to his beloved, chastising her for being unfaithful or proposing a secret tryst. Opposite: **A Cabbage Rose** from Pierre-Joseph Redouté's Les Roses, 1817.*

Rosa centifolia Bullata.
Rosier à feuilles de Laitue.

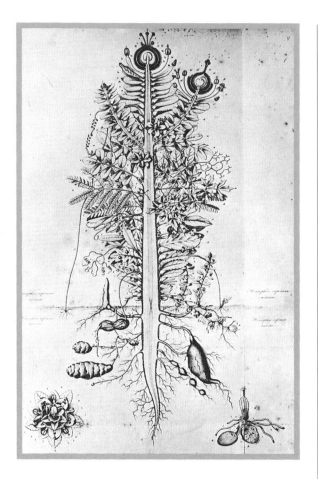

among modern herbal cures it is used to combat sterility, so that it is difficult to get to the source of it!

Provided parsley is sewn only on Good Friday, it is no longer associated with the spirit of death, and the tomato is known as the love apple – though its growth is often associated with human excrement.

As a matter of modern interest, the use of garden gnomes in homes around many parts of Europe is a replacement for the original protective gods Aphrodite and Undine. Gnomes were originally Germanic goblins who were traditional protectors of treasure, so their position today is truly important.

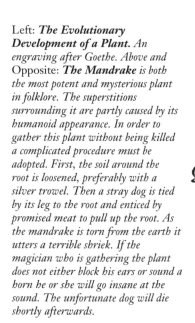

Superstition

The significance of different vegetables.

Lore and Sources

Garden vegetables also carry great and significant indications of the fates and fortunes of humans, tossed as we are within the vagaries of luck, though not always with a very great deal of logic. Lettuce, for example, was believed to be an aphrodisiac by the Romans, and in the Middle Ages in Europe, it was used in love potions. On the other hand, during the same period in Europe it was also said that if too many lettuce grew in a garden, the woman of the household would be sterile. And still today,

Left: *The Evolutionary Development of a Plant. An engraving after Goethe. Above and* Opposite: *The Mandrake is both the most potent and mysterious plant in folklore. The superstitions surrounding it are partly caused by its humanoid appearance. In order to gather this plant without being killed a complicated procedure must be adopted. First, the soil around the root is loosened, preferably with a silver trowel. Then a stray dog is tied by its leg to the root and enticed by promised meat to pull up the root. As the mandrake is torn from the earth it utters a terrible shriek. If the magician who is gathering the plant does not either block his ears or sound a horn he or she will go insane at the sound. The unfortunate dog will die shortly afterwards.*

ANIMAL CRACKERS

IT WAS SECURELY ASSERTED right up to Victorian times that animals possessed no soul and were, for all practical purposes of a much lesser value than mankind, the superior being on this planet. With the advent of the extraordinary amount of damage that man has sustained on his world, we may be less willing to place ourselves at the head of the superiority stakes today. In fact we tend now to look upon animals as having many qualities that man could learn much from, and the world of superstition is no exception.

Superstition

The psychic powers of animals.

Lore and Sources

Dogs are said to be able to tell coming death and danger and can reputedly see ghosts, while cats, in the world of mysticism, carry a far higher magical

power than ever man pretended. The origin of cat-power derives almost certainly from the original Egyptian worship of the cat emblem "Bast" in the city of Bubastes. Anyone visiting a museum of Egyptian artifacts will find the beautiful Bast cat sitting elegantly with the paws positioned perfectly in front, the dark black coloring strongly reminiscent of power and black magic. The witchcraft of the Middle Ages turned the black cat into the "familiar"; a creature that could change shape and perform or help perform rituals and spells for the witch. Today, we fear the black cat that crosses our path. This represents most clearly the conflict that existed between the Church, the cross and the pagan practices of witchcraft.

If a black cat walks towards you in America and Europe, it brings good fortune, but if it walks away, it takes the luck with it. Mothers should always keep cats away from babies because they "suck the breath" of the child like a vampire. If we watch cats while they snuggle up to us on our laps, they will tend to come close to the mouth and sniff. One can imagine how this might have seemed, given the fear of dark forces, like a sucking motion that might endanger a child by sucking out its life.

Left: *Ancient Egyptians believed cats had souls and we have the overwhelming evidence of literally millions of their mummified remains, like this example, to prove it.*
Opposite: *While it was usually a cat that was a familiar for a witch and a dog for a wizard, the concept of all totem animals has a long and persistent history.* **Girl with a Dog** *by Morris Hirshfield, Bragaline Collection, USA.*

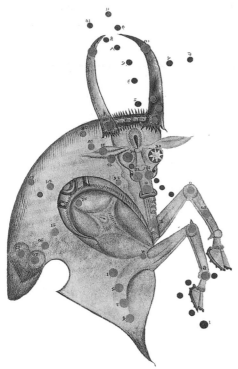

***Miniature** from a 13th c. Persian manuscript called The Book of the Stars showing the main constellations of the astrological sign of Taurus.*

Superstition

The religious significance of the cow.

Lore and Sources

The religious significance of the cow in India is well known to us all, and for anyone who has visited the country the story is more than evident as these extraordinary horned animals lope along the busiest roads, somehow managing not to be run over by a thousand rushing vehicles. In the marketplaces they are reluctantly permitted to eat the fresh vegetables that line the streets and can often even be seen to snatch food from passing baskets and from the shoulders and under the arms of the poorest shoppers. No Indian will kill a cow under any circumstances, for doing so would be to kill a reincarnated person and the act would risk bad karma for lifetimes to come. Some say that the belief also has far more practical purposes insofar as living cows go on producing milk for years while dead ones feed a family only once.

In other parts of the world there is no such concern, though the cow's milk was once believed to cure consumption, the terrible sickness that killed so many in Europe around the end of the last century.

Opposite: ***Four-leaf and chevron symbols of the goddess adorn the face of a bull.** Crete, 1600 B.C.E., British Museum* Above: ***Silver Proto-Elamite cow deity** from Iran, 2900 B.C.E., Metropolitan Museum of Art, New York.*

Magpie

There are many recorded instances of country folk being in real terror if a single pynot or "Maggotty-Pie" flew across their path. Two of the most popular rhymes concerning this dangerous bird of omen are:

One for Anger
  Two for Mirth
Three for a Wedding
  And four for a Birth
Five for Silver
  But six for Gold
Seven for a secret
  that's never been told.
Eight for Heaven
  And nine for Hell
Ten for the Devil
  Who'll get yer so'elle

One for Sorrow
  Two for Joy
Three for a Letter
  Four for a Boy
Five is for rich
  And six for Poor
Seven for a Witch
  And Eight for a Whore
Nine for a Burying
  I ca tell thee no more.

Tradition accuses the magpie of not wearing full mourning at the Crucifixion and is supposed to carry a drop of the Devil's blood under its tongue

Death's Head Hawk Moth

Sometimes a superstition arose from the principle of like-makes-like. In this case the strange, skull-like pattern on the back of the Hawk moth lent credence to a belief that it was a damned soul returned to the scene of its past. From Moses Harris's The Aurelian 1766, Natural History Museum Library, London.

Salamander

This creature is one of the most basic of alchemical symbols. Supposedly it can live within the hottest fires and its touch was thought to be fatal. Historia Naturalis Ronarum by Roesel van Rosenhof 1758.

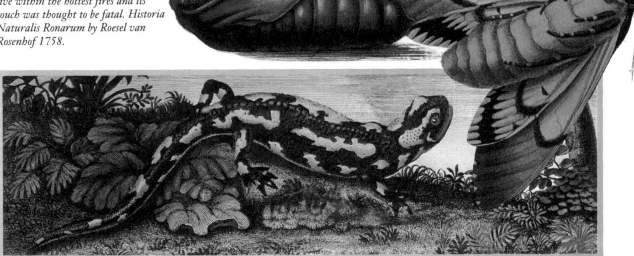

Fox

The fox has always been linked in superstition with the dark forces. Even the country folk, who should have known better, believed its bite to be fatal. Presumably its sinister reputation was fired by the raids made in the hours of darkness upon the farmers' poultry. Wood engraving by Thomas Bewick

Hedgehog

These strange little creatures are actually good news for any farmer, keeping many pestilent bugs in check. Yet they were often hunted and killed in the curious belief that they sucked milk from cows. Another odd tale suggests that they stole apples on their "prickly backs". From Buffon's Histoire Naturelle 1738

Owl

A beautiful legend in the great Celtic masterpiece, The Mabinogion, tells of a magical maiden who was fashioned from flowers by a powerful wizard for his nephew to marry. She falls in love with another man and rebels against the whole male, authoritarian rule which created her and married her off. As a punishment the wizard turns her into an owl to be shunned or attacked by all the other birds. That is why the owl only hunts at night. But she can see deeper than other creatures and her shriek is an omen of forthcoming death or bad luck for whoever hears it. A child born to the sound of an owl calling will suffer a cruel life. Virginian Eared Owl from Histoire Naturelle des Oiseaux de l'Amerique Septentio Trional 1807.

Pig

The pig or wild boar held a pride of honor within Celtic mythology and some of the legends have been transformed into the superstitions of today. Those who eat a pig's brain are thought to be incapable of telling a lie. Wood engraving by Thomas Bewick.

Swan

A swan's feather, sewed into the husband's pillow, was thought to ensure fidelity. Perhaps this custom arose from the fact that swans mate for life. There is also the widespread belief that the "swan song" of the otherwise mute swan only happens just before it dies. Wood engraving by Thomas Bewick.

Swallow

Tradition had it that swallows carry two precious stones. A red stone will cure madness and a black stone will ensure good luck.

Cock

It was a common practice in Europe and the UK that a cock would be buried in the foundations of a new building to protect it from mishap and evil. The unfortunate birds were also buried at the junction of three streams or at a crossroads to avert evil or cure disease. Wood engraving by Thomas Bewick.

Cockatrice

Such legendary creatures were once as famous as dragons and Elephants in Europe. Supposedly a magical cock's egg was incubated by a toad resulting in a fearful winged monster which, once fully grown, began to eat people. There is a surprising amount of literature and written evidence surrounding the tale of a man from Harewood Forest in Southern England who eventually killed the infamous Wherwell Cockatrice by tricking it to fight its own reflection from a mirror which he lowered into the monster's lair. Once it was exhausted the hero rushed in and destroyed it. Right: The weather Cock-atrice which once adorned the church steeple at Wherwell.

SAINT CHRISTOPHER'S CURSE

THE AUTOMOBILE HAS BECOME one of the most potent shrines of modern man and with its ability to bring power, prestige, and death it carries a plethora of mystical values which we cannot ignore.

Superstition

Never boast that you have had no accidents.

Lore and Sources

To boast good fortune will surely bring about bad fortune. In the lore of superstition this is known as tempting providence, and derives from the concept of like will produce like or unlike. The origin of this comes to us from the ancient Greek myths in which it was believed that the gods watched everything that mankind did, and if he became too confident then it was time to give him a nasty shock. As a result of this belief many precautions would need to be taken to keep out of the view of the gods.

Superstition

Matters to be observed in your choice of vehicle.

Lore and Sources

Don't buy a new car on Friday the 13th (see "The Threshold of Belief") for obvious reasons, or the vehicle will spend most of its time in the hands of the mechanic. If you acquire a car which works well and causes no problems, continue to always buy the same brand for "changing the car, changes your luck." Accidents always run in threes, so watch out especially after the second one. If you are fortunate to be wealthy enough to buy a holy man's car, you will inherit his holiness. Remember

to wash the car every Saturday for then, for sure it will rain on Sunday! The reason is simple. If you imitate an event, it will be bound to happen. Primitive rain-makers have been successful in this for thousands of years.

There is a huge market today for personalized number plates which, although in America can be made specially by the licensing authorities, throughout Europe must be purchased at great cost. The most popular numbers are the lucky numbers 3, 7, 9 which being odd numbers are under the protection of the gods themselves.

Superstition

That Saint Christopher protects travellers.

Lore and Sources

Poor Saint Christopher, the embattled protector of all travellers, has had a hard time during this century but still remains one of the most popular saints in our hallowed world of superstition. The original Saint Christopher, before his martyrdom, asked God that wherever his body lay, that place would be protected from pestilence and "mischiefs". It became a tradition therefore for pictures of him to be placed in public places and at the entrances of towns and churches on the understanding that "if you see Saint Christopher, you will be safe."

Above: **St. Christopher** *from a Westminster Psalter. Royal mss.*
Right: *The tradition of Good Luck charms for newly weds remains a firm favorite even today.*

CHAPTER THREE

RATING THE IRRATIONAL

Left: *Drawing by Levi who is demonstrating the hidden fact that
Satan is really only a reflection of God or the shadow of the deity.*
Opposite: *A magical design by J. F. C. Fuller.*

WE CAN APPRECIATE BY NOW that the basic essences of superstition arose originally out of a deep respect for and fear of magic.

Both fear and magic engender great confusion in our minds, particularly because they are not rational. There is nothing sensible or ordered in the world of the wizard. So in this chapter, instead of concentrating on one subject area and behaving in a rational and reasonable fashion, we are going to take a closer look at the more bizarre and unlikely beliefs that find their places among our normal lives today; the unlikely nature of the superstitions being the only connecting point of the chapter.

THE ROYAL, THE REGAL, THE NATION, AND THE FLAG

THE HUMAN DYNASTY HAS LONG HELD its "upper-crust" in awe, originally through a belief that God appointed a single representative to be the earthly ruler of each country (or originally each area or state). In France, for example, the King was in effect God incarnate and had absolute power over all other human beings under his command. Men and women are willing to go to war and die for their "King and Country" and the flag that represents the nation forms an important emblem of loyalty and must be guarded against loss.

Originally, the sovereign of the state had to undergo the most powerful rituals, and if we look back at early kings like Arthur, Ethelred the Unready, and the mythical rulers such as Neptune and Zeus the degree of magic surrounding their anointed position as head of humanity or country illustrates the beliefs and superstitions of humanity with an aura that is close to the most divine magic.

Right: ***The Raven Master*** *at the Tower of London.* Left: ***Raven*** *by Audobon, Natural History Museum Library, London.*

Superstition

The powers that maintain the monarchy.

Lore and Sources

Among the many superstitions that surround the monarchs of all ages, there are some that have long lost their meaning, such as the falling of a crop of ash keys, the winged seeds of the ash tree, which was once thought to forebode the coming death of the monarch.

Perhaps one of the most odd and yet also picturesque of the royal protection superstitions lies in the wings of the ravens that reside in and around the parapets of the Tower of London. The ancient lore states that should they decide to leave, the British monarchy will fall. They have been in the vicinity of the Tower since before the time of Henry VIII and for the past few centuries their presence has been assured by good food, plentiful attention and the judicious clipping of their wings.

Superstition

Royal jewellry, and the sovereign or state crown holds special magical powers.

Lore and Sources

The crown and scepter, still used in England to celebrate and inaugurate the new King or Queen, are derived from the nimbus of the most ancient Sun God, a garland surrounding the monarch with a bejewelled halo of light and power and the magician's wand. Kings, only two hundred years in our past, were believed to possess healing powers, and with the laying on of hands they could cure "the King's Evil," a disease also known as scrofula, and one that brought unpleasant swellings in the throat. Beneath the monarch's throne in England, the Coronation stone has rested for hundreds of years as a symbol of supernatural powers that protect the seated sovereign and the nation against evil.

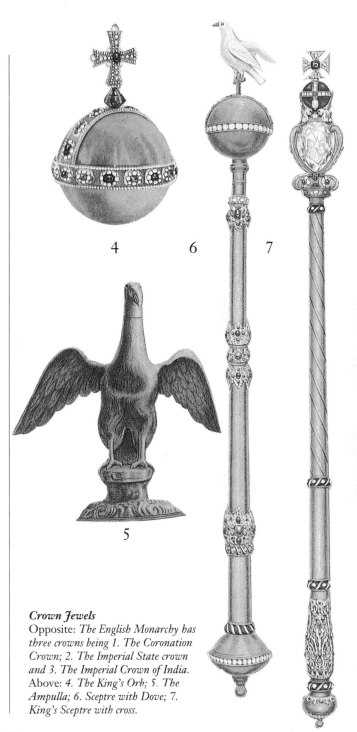

4   6   7

5

Crown Jewels
Opposite: *The English Monarchy has three crowns being 1. The Coronation Crown; 2. The Imperial State crown and 3. The Imperial Crown of India.* Above: *4. The King's Orb; 5. The Ampulla; 6. Sceptre with Dove; 7. King's Sceptre with cross.*

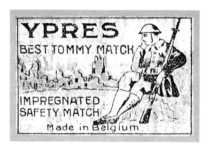

Right: *Tattoo designs from 1940. A Recruitment poster for 1916 showing the legendary St. George of England fighting the Dragon. Such is the power of nationalistic superstitions and traditional beliefs of superiority that such obviously bogus images can still incite a warlike stance. Left: The superstition that to light the third cigarette from the same match is the worst of luck most likely had its source in the trenches of Flanders and France in 1914 to 1918. An enemy sniper would be able to take aim and fire in the darkness at any light held for more than a few seconds.*

Superstition

The rites and practises of war.

Lore and Sources

During the wars fought between nations, the variety and primitive nature of superstition makes for the most unlikely stories. During World War II, Hitler hired astrologers to predict the outcome and progress of the war, and in order to combat his primitive instincts the British did the same. The respective propaganda organizations decided that to make the best of the situation and respectively rally or destroy the confidence of the home and away "teams" they would hire airplanes to drop leaflets over the opposing cities with scurrilous material which blackened both Hitler and Churchill's names in the light of the advice of the planets!

When a country goes to war, it effectively submits to the tribal god and under that protection sets out to murder its fellow men across the water with the battle cry that was originally that of human sacrifice. In effect there is no difference between war and ancient sacrifice. The most primitive societies of the past, a man was chosen from the local tribe or village and taken into the fields, where he was cut up into small pieces and spread across the land to appease the gods of the harvest and land so that the coming season would produce adequate food and goods. In the same way, war is an appeasement of the gods that protect our nations and our lands against the evil foreigner.

During World War II many people would carry rabbit's feet continuously which they would rub in their hands fervently when forced to walk through the streets at night, believing that this determined use of magical energy would draw good luck from the charm into their luckless bodies.

On the other end of the scale, the soldier who goes into battle will cover his body in good-luck charms and talismans, such as lucky pennies, hare's or rabbit's feet, necklaces, pictures of loved ones and survive under the belief that there is perhaps only one bullet "with my name on it," and until that arrives he is safe.

But why the rabbit's foot? What did the poor innocent rabbit do in our distant past to carry the responsibility of having such magic in its foot?

HARE TODAY, GONE TOMORROW

Superstition

The luck of the rabbit's foot.

Lore and Sources

The earliest derivation of this strange tradition actually arises not from the rabbit but from the hare. Witches of the twelfth century in Wales were witnessed to have changed themselves into hares in order to suck the milk of pregnant mothers! It might be hard for modern mothers to imagine that there was a time when a woman would even think of allowing an animal to take her milk, but in the rural areas of medieval Europe it wasn't unusual for a small peasant household to contain not only the whole family of dozens of children, but the animals also, living right there in the home. Goats, cows, pigs, hares, rabbits, chickens, and ducks were all welcomed into the home (or hovel) because the conditions of climate and general welfare made it necessary for the people to find warmth by whatever means available. There was no heating and very little light, so the family took advantage of animal body heat to booster against the cold.

Hares were bred for eating and cared for with almost the same concern as a child, except

that a pregnant mother could derive greater benefit from an animal's warmth against her body than a baby. While sitting comfortably in a corner of the home, the mother would cuddle the hare and allow it to suckle from her breast. The phrase, "Hare, hare, God send the care," was commonly spoken when the hunt was on in the forests and lands of the rural areas of England to catch the large population of the animal for the aristocratic dinner table. Witch hunts and hare-hunts went hand in hand, and the belief was that the witch would turn herself into a hare temporarily and sneak into a peasant home for safety.

A hare, once caught, might prove difficult to skin or to cook, and this would lead the cook to believe that the animal had transformed into a witch before death.

As far back as the time of the ancient Britons, before Rome conquered the British Isles, hares were considered magical creatures to be used in the rituals surrounding divination, and in books of the time it is plainly stated that the animal should not be eaten at all because of its magical qualities.

Meeting a hare on a May morning is particularly unlucky, and the only way to combat the coming bad fortune is to spit over your left shoulder and utter the words, "Hare before, Trouble behind: Change ye, Cross, and free me." Or touch each shoulder with a forefinger and say the words, "Hare, hare, God send thee care."

The idea of the hare's foot as a lucky charm also arose out of the primitive medical belief that the bone of a hare's foot cured gout and cramp, though the bone had to be one with a joint in it intact, to be effective. Carrying a hare's foot bone, with joint, would keep away all forms of rheumatism.

The hare and the rabbit, being so similar in appearance, were joined together as a development of the superstitions surrounding their medical and magical qualities. Seamen would not utter the word rabbit on board ship because of its associations with fortune. Mothers would put a rabbit's foot into the cradle of the newborn baby, having brushed the child's forehead with the foot shortly after birth in a kind of baptismal ritual.

But the truth is, if we believe in the power of time to imbue an object with luck, that it is the hare's foot that has built up the energy and not the poor rabbit's for the rabbit that lost its foot cannot be called so lucky.

Right: *The Hare from The Hunting Book by Gaston Phoebus, 14th c.*
Left: *A "cony" in Elizabethan times was a country innocent or a dupe who was easily preyed upon by confidence tricksters who tempted the gullible to part with their money.*

THE GRIM REAPER AND HIS FRIENDS

CONTINUING WITH OUR STORY of the more unlikely superstitions, we can jump to some very bizarre, and in some ways poetic derivations that center on death and affliction – two human conditions that attract the highest degree of fear and magic. And what more powerful machine exists today to carry fear and magic than the ambulance?

Superstition

When an ambulance passes, death and affliction are in the air.

Lore and Sources

Although we have a very practical purpose in making ambulances extremely noisy and powerful, there is a strong and quite old background to their position in our social belief systems. We get out of the way of an ambulance instinctively, we say, because the dying must be given free passage to recovery, but perhaps there is also something deeper in our group memories that brings about such a reaction to that screaming sound in the street.

At the turn of the century in England it was said that children in London would turn up their coat collars on seeing an ambulance and call out the words, "Grab your collar, don't swaller, never catch the fever." Or, "There goes the fever-van, never touch the mealy-man." The ritual included holding your breath and pinching your nose until you saw a black or brown dog. A young girl was heard to cry, "Touch your toes, touch your nose, never go in one of those. Hold your collar, do not swallow until you see a dog."

If we remember that not so long ago, most of Europe was beset by a disease so terrible that it killed more than half of the populations of many cities and rural areas, it becomes clear from where this superstition and its attendant incantations arose. The dreaded Black Death or "pestilence", bubonic plague, attacked the human world on and off for hundreds of years between the twelfth and seventeenth centuries. It arrived, supposedly, from China in a boat that docked on the island of Sicily, filled with dead sailors who lay in the most gruesome condition on the boards of the deck, covered in pussing boils. The plague raged from there through southern Europe and into France, where it killed hundreds of thousands of people, sometimes within hours of its arrival in an area. One of the most dramatic periods of the plague occurred in the early sixteenth century in Provence, when people were said to sew themselves inside death shawls to await their own deaths because there was no one around to do it for them after death.

The common belief was that the disease was somehow carried in the air and could be breathed in by anyone, so little or nothing was done to combat it's actual transmission through the generally dreadful conditions of life: excrement in the streets; rats and mice in the homes; poor diet with a lack of vitamins and other nutritious content. The clergy of the once Papal city of Naples burned huge bonfires throughout the streets of the city in the belief that this would somehow set fire to the plague that floated through the air. The device worked, though for other reasons: the fires had to be fed with materials to keep them lit and local people cast in their old furniture, garbage, and dirty clothes, disposing of the items that helped carry the disease among them.

We need only take a short jump from the idea that diseases are carried in the air, to the "fever-van" that makes a young child turn up his collar against the cold to reduce the resistance to disease. He holds the breath and pinches the nose against germs and looks for a dog that will absorb it instead. The word mealy, as in mealy-man, means spotty – covered in the spots brought about by infectious disease. So watch out for the ambulances, but don't hold your breath for too long.

Triumph of Death, Palerma, 15th c. The
Grim Reaper with Sythe and Bow strikes down
both old and young, rich and poor in the great
Plague which decimated Europe in three
horrendous years.

APPLE-SEEDS AND FINGERTIPS

JUMPING FROM AMBULANCES TO APPLES, we continue to be unreasonable when we discover that the simple appleseed has a plethora of traditions surrounding its existence. Why? Because the very earliest of human beings, about eight to ten thousand years ago, was tempted out of the Garden of Eden by an apple.

Superstition

Incantations with an apple for finding a lover.

But before getting to the seed, we can have some fun with the peel. Take the fresh new apple in your hand and peel it with a knife. Hold the peel in your right hand and say the words:
> "St. Simon and St. Jude, on you I intrude,
> By this paring I hold to discover,
> Without any delay, to tell me this day,
> The first letter of my own true lover."

Then turn around three times and cast the peel over your left shoulder (avoiding hitting the devil). The shape in which the peel lands on the ground is the first letter of the name you seek. Alternatively, you must peel the apple without a break in the peel, hang it behind the door of the house, and the first initial of the name of the first person to come into the house thereafter will be the initial of the name of the one you will marry.

Now you may eat the apple, but keep the seeds, for these must be thrown into the fire with the words, "If you love me, pop and fly, if you hate me, lay and die," while at the same time you name an imaginary lover whose desire you wish to test.

Still more seeds are needed to find true love (presuming that the above didn't work), so take one between the thumb and forefinger and flick it off into the distance, saying:

> "Kernel come kernel, hop over my thumb,
> And tell me which way my truelove will come,
> East, west, north or south,
> Kernel jump into my true love's mouth."

The anxious inquirer is said to move round in a circle, squeezing the apple seed until it shoots away in the direction of the lover's home. Once the seed has departed continue with:

> "Pippin, pippin, paradise,
> Tell me where my true love lies;
> East, west, north or south,
> Pilling brig, or Cocker-mouth."

There is no clear translation or derivation of "Pilling brig or Cocker-mouth," except that a brig was the place on a boat where the sailors slept and Cocker-mouth is almost certainly a place in England which probably eventually became Cockermouth. As we mentioned at the beginning of this

chapter, it is not always necessary to know the facts about the past, feelings may sometimes be enough.

Returning to the apple seeds, if you are not too good at aiming things, then the ritual can be made simpler by placing the seed in the palm of the hand, covering it with the other hand and shaking it around while repeating the incantations above. When the hands are open, the seed will be pointing in the right direction.

What fun can be had, and to what effect with a simple seed and a fingertip!

Lovers on a grassy seat by the Master E.S. circa 1450.

THE CROSS OF AGES

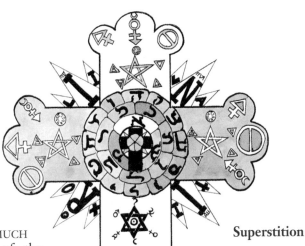

WE CANNOT GO TOO MUCH FURTHER along the route of the irrational without coming into intimate contact with the cross.

The cross is associated most directly with Jesus Christ, but it was around as a symbol long before Christianity was even a glimmer in the eyes of the Church, and did not appear in Christian art until six hundred years after the death of Christ. As with other religious symbols that we have already discussed, the cross was adopted by the Christian Church as part of its campaign to incorporate all that was most precious to humanity, as though it were its own. Early Christians in fact counted the cross as a pagan symbol and therefore repudiated it. Father Minucius Felix in the third century indignantly denied that Christians worshipped the cross, saying, "You it is, ye Pagans, who are the most likely people to adore wooden crosses...for what else are your ensigns, flags, and standards, but crosses gilt and beautiful. Your victorious trophies not only represent a simple cross, but a cross with a man on it."

Left: ***Christ of John of the Cross*** *by Salvador Dali.*
Above: ***The Red Cross***, *the emblem of the Order of the Golden dawn. This synthesis of many cultures and traditions includes the 22 letters of the Hebrew alphabet, the 22 paths of the Tree of Life, the five-petalled Calvary cross and the 4 armed cross of nature.*

Superstition

The practice of using the cross for all manner of fears and beliefs. Crossing the body, the fingers, the heart.

The practice of crossing oneself as an act of worship or against uncertainty is so common that we hardly give it a thought. Each time we make a promise that we fear we may not keep, we cross our fingers against failure. Each time we wish for something that we fear may not happen, we cross our fingers. Each time we look for good luck, the most common gesture is crossing the fingers. We cross our heart "and hope to die" as a gesture of trust. The cross appears even in our roads, and in fact has great significance in magical and superstitious terms because we think of a crossroads as significant, both in traffic and in our lives. So why the passion for the cross, and how long has it been around?

Lore and Sources

If we remember yet again the concept of the necessity of sacrificing a man for the continued good harvest, we can easily understand the cross with a crucified man on it standing in a field, later to be symbolised with a wooden sculpture of the same. This was in no way the exclusive symbolism of

Jesus on the Cross. In fact, it is often suggested by anthropologists and theologians that the symbol of Jesus on the Cross and the whole process of crucifying him in this primitive manner was no more than mankind sacrificing one of his greatest saviors to the future "harvest" of humanity as a whole.

Today we sacrifice the scarecrow in the field to chase away the marauding birds as a last vestige of the crucified King whose pagan blood would fertilize the earth, even though we know for sure that no crow could care less for a stuffed jacket on a pole.

The cross also appeared in Celtic mythology with a circle around the center to symbolize a combination of the phallus and the female genital circle or oval, thus signifying marriage between the sexes. This sign was also know to the Hindus as the "Kiakra", a male-female sign of sexual union (it is believed that the Celts and the Hindus were once one tribe that split and went opposite ways). The male cross and the female orb also composed the Egyptian "amulet Nefer" or blessed amulet, the charm of sexual harmony thousands of years ago.

There are even crosses, found mostly from Celtic areas of Europe, that are shaped exactly like a penis, with a realistic "meatus" (penis-head) at the top of the cross. The Christians fathers didn't like this in some parts of the world so that it was sanded down to reduce the obvious implications.

All the way back to pre-Columbian times in the West, there were crosses carried by "saviors" symbolizing sacrifice and suffering on behalf of mankind in the same style as Jesus of Nazareth.

There is no certain date when Christianity actually adopted the cross as a symbol connected with Jesus. The original Hermetic Christians were actually less violent in their associations, depicting Jesus carrying a lamb rather than a large hunk of wood, thereby connecting Godliness with the earth – Jesus being the "Good Shepherd." Once the cross was adopted it not only appeared as the traditional Latin cross that we have today but in the more ancient forms of the Greek cross of equal arms, the X-shaped cross from St. Andrew, the Gnostic Maltese cross, the solar cross or cross of Wotan, a version of the Egyptian "ankh" or Cross of Venus, and even the swastika taken up by the Nazis in Hitler's era.

The connection between the cross and the male and female genitals is probably the true origin, for even the ancient Greek Goddess Isis is depicted carrying a cross in one hand on the Isiac Table, the other hand holding a lotus seed vessel, thus signifying male and female genitals.

Druid priests used a headless T-shaped cross called a "Tau-Cross" made by stripping oak trees of their branches and then strapping large tree limbs to the top to represent arms. This cross was originally employed as the May Day cross, and the English still use a derivative of this to dance around and criss-cross with the strands that run from the top in a kind of modern version of the original fertility rituals, though the English Maypole is actually of a different origin in fact.

The Christian "True Cross" has been the source of a number of bizarre stories, particularly connected to the nails, the INRI sign that was nailed to the top, and splinters of the cross itself. There are enough "genuine" holy splinters from the original cross to make several hundred crosses! Pope Alexander III decreed positively that the Holy Nails and the INRI sign were in the hands of the Church of Rome. The splinters, scattered into the hands of numerous priests and church authorities, have been used for centuries as holy relics with various powers to heal and cure.

The same Church claimed that the True Cross was made from the same wood that grew as the Tree of Life in the Garden of Eden. Adam carried it out when he was banished and kept it for the Christian patriarchs, who even managed to take it aboard Noah's Ark during the Flood. Somehow the wood was sustained and used, according to legend, to crucify Jesus a few thousand years later, all purposefully planned.

Tree of Life and Death by Berthold Furtmeyer, 1481.

The Gnostics added their own complexity to this extraordinary story of justification by stating that the True Cross on which Jesus died was made by his father, Joseph the Carpenter, and that it was planted in Golgotha in exactly the spot where the Tree of Life had grown. Such stories were the basis of religious dogma during hundreds of years.

And going back surely to near the very beginning of the cross symbol we find that during Neolithic times, the original labyrinth design (there is only one that existed all over the world in different cultures) contained a cross that penetrated through the opening as a male/female genital symbol. These designs can still be found in Tintagel in England, at Chartres Cathedral in France, and Weir Island in Finland.

The cross turns up, of course, in many other forms throughout the normal everyday life of humanity, particularly as the crossroads. Travellers would make offerings to the sprite Hecate of the Three Ways who had three faces, and festivals called Compitalia were enjoyed around roadside shrines at crossroads.

It is now firmly believed that energy lines called "leys" exist across America (also Europe and China) which run a few feet below the surface of the ground, and are detectable by electro-magnetic sensors. These leys have, it is suggested, been cre-

Above: *A handle of a bucket from the Oseberg ship burial. Saxon.* Opposite: *Slab glass ceiling of Blackwood Hall, Melbourne, Australia by the stained glass artist, Leonard French.*

ated by the constant passage of men and animals between various important places, such as towns and villages, or churches, on foot or horse, to and fro, over hundreds and thousands of years. They have been detected between points where special shrines have been set up by the American Indians at crossroads between them, in the same way as the European ancients did. They were areas for weary travellers and places of worship to see them on their way. This was, in fact, the very basis of the original crossroads, so that it wasn't simply a matter of roads crossing one another, but a religious significance was built into the convergence and related both to the cross and a place of rest and meditation.

The most ancient pagan rites took place at crossroads for the celebration of what we would today regard as black magic – though in the earliest days, black and white were one. Mothers would take their children to the "crossways" and drag them across the ground as a ritual sacrifice to Mother Earth or to make them the children of the Devil.

A more recent manifestation of the darker side of superstitious magic brings the cross and the crossroad together in the form of the gibbet, the cross on which criminals and witches were hung during medieval times – the corpse being buried in the unhallowed ground beside the road.

THE PSYCHIC AND THE DIVINE

STICKING FIRMLY TO OUR IRRATIONAL and meandering pattern, we enter now into one of the most fascinating aspects of superstition, and one that has survived longer than any other. One that in America has even grown to prominence during the last few decades, particularly on the West Coast.

Superstition

That the human "mind" or some other aspect of – the human body, possesses the power to enact certain psychic functions that cannot be explained rationally. These include psychic surgery, clairvoyance, extra sensory perception and many other functions that exist somewhere between superstition and mysticism.

Lore and Sources

In New York during the 1960s a Brazilian "psychic surgeon" named Luroval was invited by Francis Huxley, the eminent anthropologist, to perform his "arts" in the presence of scientists. During the sessions he would go into a trance with the aid of a guitar and half a bottle of whiskey, and then proceed to remove tumors from various parts of various guests without anaesthetic – in one case using a pair of scissors and a blunt razor. A photographer took pictures of the "operations" which were subsequently published in a book on the subject (now unavailable) which attempted to prove the existence of this extraordinary practice.

Lyall Watson, the biologist and occultist, has spent his life traveling around the more obscure countries of the world witnessing these primitive psychic activities and publishing his findings in various entertaining and imaginative volumes such as "Supernature", his first and most popular book.

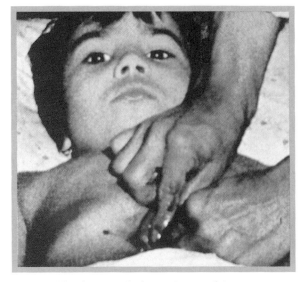

Whether we believe in psychic powers or not, the most interesting feature of them is that they all tend to be sourced in the most ancient lore and have their roots firmly within the same ground as superstition, magic, and mysticism, all of which derived from the very beginning of time. Clairvoyance, tarot reading, palm reading, prophecy, and faith healing are all born out of basic principles of voice, touch, gesture, and symbolic relationships between mankind, animals, and the earth. We might observe that the practices of "witchcraft" which gave life to group expertise such as clairvoyance and the old faith-healing professions were performed for the definite purpose of finding mystical power, whereas the individual superstitions that we have sampled in this book so far were more to do with a kind of self defense against the vagaries of uncertainty and fate. Nevertheless, they all grow from the same basic lores.

Left: *Psychic surgeons often use the most primitive of tools with which to operate. Complex tumors and other growths are removed painlessly, with open wounds healing within a few moments. It is difficult to distinguish between the fake and the true healer but many patients claim remarkable and even miraculous cures.* Right: **Scene from the Travels of Sir John Mandeville.** *Many of the occult or esoteric mysteries which were practised in the Dark Ages have retained their popularity, judging from the Astrological predictions which can be found in virtually every newspaper and magazine of today. Under this deluge of Sun signs, charts and future predictions it is difficult to judge fairly if there is any truth in the so called Science of the Stars or whether it is just the biggest hoax in the big business boom of selling superstitions.*

Another experience that may be enjoyed still today is a visit to an Italian clairvoyant named Vera Chiesa (True Church) in Turin, during which this diminutive woman uses an ancient Ouija board and while, in a kind of trance, gets in touch with "the spirits" to discover past lives and messages from "the beyond."

In both cases, with the Brazilian healer and the Italian clairvoyant, the most evident aspect of the performances was the similarity of the methods to those practiced by ancient shamanic witch-doctors and priests. Incantations, lowering of the voice, dark lighting, and the use of deep trance were employed to find the connections between the rational "reality" that twentieth century man is so proud of and the darker forces of the irrational that somehow have managed to survive the scientific age.

In certain rural parts of England and very much in California and New Mexico (though perhaps on a more commercial footing) many of the practicing psychics employ tools of trade that have been around for years. Crystalomancy – the use of transparent objects such as globes, crystals, and mirrors – is still very popular, and the ancient superstition of standing before a mirror at night and watching to see the future lover appear in the glass is still practiced by hopeful singles.

In the earlier part of this century, Carl Gustav Jung, an Austrian Psychiatrist, proposed and wrote about ways in which dreams could be used to define deep areas of the human unconscious. This seemingly revolutionary method of interpretation has strongly influenced the medical world ever since, but its source lies deeply embedded in ancient folklore, familiar as far back into history as ancient Greece under the name of "oneirocritica," the study of dreaming.

Dactyliomancy, the practice of suspending a gold or other metal ring on a piece of twine and allowing it to swing over a round table covered in letters of the alphabet will tell the enquirer about any number of likely trends in the future. Pregnant women will take a wedding ring, tie it with a piece of cotton and allow it to swing over the belly. If the ring swings from one side to the other, the child is said to be a boy. If the swinging is circular, it is said to be a girl.

The more commercial version of dactyliomancy is the use of the Ouija board or planchette where any number of strange answers may be achieved from the spirit world through what was originally called "sciomancy", or "the calling up of names of the deceased to give the intelligence of things to come."

Above: ***Owl***, *from a design by William De Morgan 1880, Victoria and Albert museum Library, London. The 'Spirit-bird', shunned by all other birds.*
Opposite: *Superstitions are fundamentally the interplay of the forces of light and darkness, good and ill fortune. Many center around the female. Today, it is a matter of opinion whether the so-called sin of disobedience which Eve committed is fact or superstition. But the central issue here is that it was the female who first sinned and who was the initiator of Adam. That dark and mysterious side of the female was a favorite subject of the Pre-Raphaelite painters of Victorian England. The painting is of the sorceress,* **Queen Eleanor and the innocent Fair Rosamund** *by Evelyn De Morgan. Here are the two aspects of the female - the witch and the good virgin.*

J.F.C.Fuller reveals the polarity of the female zodiacal circle being penetrated by the male forces of the material world. Harry Price Collection, University of London.

Here "Boney" Fuller offers a design for an occult and magical temple which was to have been built but never materialised.

All this modern and ancient acceptance of the unlikely and unprovable arises directly out of the proposed existence of supernatural forces, and our willingness to accept them because of our human superstitious attitude to life. We don't know, so we prefer to cover the odds.

The same potentially deep reverence exists today within western minds for the eastern guru. A huge increase in the number of disciples of cult religions has been seen in the past two or three decades with religious masters such as Osho Rajneesh, J.Krishnamurti and Da Free John. Thousands of people travel to India and the Far East to sit at the feet of enlightened individuals who adhere to the concept of reincarnation.

Reincarnation and other spiritual practices presume an afterlife existence with a spirit world that has a powerful hold over mankind. In other words, if we accept such philosophies we also accept dimensions of existence beyond the everyday life of humanity on Earth, beyond the evident range of the simple five senses.

The truth is that a very large proportion of humanity has, at one time or another, undergone personal experiences which can only be described as psychic. And the most fascinating aspect of this is that it does not appear to matter what the tool of the experience might be – tarot cards, tea-leaf reading, palm reading – for the mystical powers of prediction, character reading, or extra-sensory

Symbolic design used by the initiates of the Rosicrucian group of the Hermetic Order of the Golden Dawn. Drawn by Moina MacGregor and in the collection of Caroline Legerman.

Another design for a projected Crowleyan Temple by Fuller. Harry Price Collection

experience derive from within the individual; the devices used being only a kind of aid to the ability.

Rituals form a strong part of these various supernatural activities. In an ashram in India, the disciples, before entering the temple of the Master, must wash themselves completely so that no unnatural odor exists on the body. They wear white robes and sit in the lotus meditation position while listening to chanting music that encourages a state of trance and calm. The arms are raised in a primitive gesture of surrender while the entire group of perhaps two thousand people will shout in unison at the entrance of the man whom they love. The entire process is reminiscent of the oldest forms of worship and ritual dating back to pre-history, unchanged during all that time.

In other areas of spiritual activity, clairvoyant gatherings will always sit in circles of twelve people – never thirteen – and hold hands around a table to summon the spirits. The chosen medium will become a vessel for the dead and provide the others in the gathering with oracular messages to direct their lives. Psychometrists will take an object of some significance to the subject and touch it against the forehead, "feeling" the story that lies behind its history and giving answers to questions. There are even examples of psychics using the power of the sun and moon to derive information not normally available to humanity.

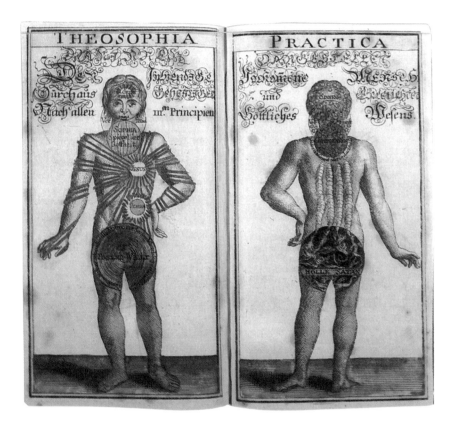

In all this there is a clear connection between what is going on in the minds and hearts of the practicing spiritual attendants and witchcraft itself, the deepest form of superstition from our past. Witches were the most superstitious people, performing the majority of their activities based on ancient lore, and acting purely out of the realms of the irrational.

And if we should wish to bring all of the above together in one profound superstitious symbol, the eastern guru, the psychic, the clairvoyant, the palmist, the astrologer, it would have to be the divine circle. Wherever we find magic or mysticism we find the circle, and of all symbols the circle forms the center and the circumference of our greatest superstitions. We live and breathe in cycles of life, energy, and magic. Magicians would always perform their magic and incantations within a specially drawn circle. The greatest earthly kings and queens would invariably have a circular inscription somewhere within their palaces or temples. The eastern masters gather their disciples together within circular halls, and spiritual groups will invariably sit together, hand in hand in a circular

fashion. We might even suggest that of all superstitious symbols there is only really one that covers all the ground, the shape of the planet Earth.

And as a last word in this chapter of the bizarre, we might take a brief look at one of the most enduring and popular (unpopular) superstitions alive today.

Opposite: ***Treatise on theoretical alchemy**, 18th c.* Above: ***Talismans**. Frontispiece painting by the magician Francis Barrett in the collection of Francis King.*

Superstition

Friday the 13th is always unlucky.

Lore and Sources

We explored in an earlier chapter, the stories surrounding the number 13 and its ill-fated beliefs, but here we can examine its most notorious application.

The superstition surrounding the fear of Friday the 13th is made up of a strange selection of different elements, which have somehow come together to focus on one single day. Why Friday?

"Now Friday came, you old wives say,
Of all the week's the unluckiest day."

This short rhyme dates from the 17th century and even before that, in Chaucer's time (1300s), the worst day of the week was always held to be a Friday. The origin, of course, is Christian, and the death of Jesus which is said to have occurred on a Friday, but the story appears to have been intensified by a certain Captain Friday who evidently, unwisely, broke every rule in the superstitions lore book. Not only did he refuse to have a gold coin laid beneath the mast of his new ship, but he also refused to have the traditional red ribbon tied to the first nail in the building of it. Worse than all this, which might have been excused through ignorance of sea-lore, Captain Friday allowed the building to commence on a Friday. In fact, he insisted on it. And the final insult, which no doubt confirmed his fate, was that he begun his maiden voyage in the ship . . . on a Friday! Needless to say, he and his ship were never seen again.

Old seamens' wisdom decrees that sailors are so superstitious that they believe no ship should be launched in a week with a Friday in it or a month with a 13th. Opposite: *Detail from* **The New York Ballance Dry Docks** *by Jurgen Frederick Huge. Collection Mr. and Mrs Jacob Kaplan.* Above: *Woodcut by Reynolds Stone.*

NEW-YORK BALLANCE DRYDOCK.

CHAPTER FOUR

All Work and No Play

Early morning commuters arriving for work on a Monday morning in the City of London.

Above: ***Postenkill, New York: Winter 1865*** *by Joseph H. Hidley, Abby Aldrich Rockefeller Folk Art Center, Williamsburg, Virginia.*

Opposite page: ***The Seal of the United States*** *reveals no less than eight groups of thirteen symbols including arrows, feathers and the stars and stripes. This number, unlucky for some, represents the original 13 states.*

NEW WORLD SUPERSTITION

ALMOST ALL OF THE SUPERSTI-
TIONS that we have encountered
so far can be applied interna-
tionally. There are very few of
us, wherever we live, that are not
aware of the dangers of the number 13 or the doubts surrounding
ladders and umbrellas, spilled salt
or milk. The whole of mankind, after
all, has grown in one way or another
from the loins of those that set up the lore
and sources in the most ancient times; those mystical and unknown wizards and peasants, witches,
and magicians that brought our fundamental fears
to the surface.

But the "new world" that we are all now
entering and which began growing in the United
States only a few hundred years ago, might seem to
be a place for the continued existence of the oldest
lores. Its very existence is supposedly based on
mankind's most modern technology and attitudes,
which would seem in contrast to ignorance and
superstition. But in fact, with even the most superficial glance, we quickly see that this is not at all
true and the "new age" of America and Europe is
one of the greatest for doubt and fear.

It may be that our determination to master
nature and create the land of the holy "dollar" has
at the same time created one of the mightiest forms
of insecurity and anxiety, so that a few million rabbit's feet would come in useful to counterbalance
these modern fears. We might expect superstition
to readily flourish in areas where social depression
and disinheritance are the norm, but it is much
stranger to discover that where economic privilege

and political power are the order
of the day, the number of irrational beliefs are greater still.
Among the rich and successful
of the west coast of the US, for
example, the magical and mystical rides higher above the waves
than in any other part of the world.
Here clairvoyance, tarot, astrology,
crystal gazing, and all the other pagan
rites and beliefs of the past line up for a
position in the public eye. If we look more closely
at the political scenes of the past few decades, com-
munism has brought the American capitalist
philosophy almost to its knees with anxiety in the
form of the "red devil" that McCarthy literally
died of (modern doctors have established that
McCarthy suffered from major stress-related heart
disease probably due to his internal physiological
and psychological anguish).

One of the most popular historical charac-
ters today is Nostradamus, whose books of predictions have achieved their greatest successes in
America; a modern land where mankind has
embraced rational thought and scientific understanding as the pillars of social order. Nostradamus
can certainly be numbered among the most primitive of seers, attaining his prophetic abilities largely through his irrational beliefs in magic, religion,
alchemy, and dark forces. For modern civilized
countries this would seem like the wildest of con-
tradictions, until we realize that we are not essentially rational at all, but deeply religious and
intensely instinctive beings – especially when it
comes to our work and play.

THE LUCK OF THE DRAW

THE BUSINESSPERSON, working and often dwelling in the city, dealing within the intensity and uncertainty of a world which truly can never be predicted, is essentially a gambler, and there is no more superstitious individual in the world than one who throws the dice.

The tensions and anxieties, the excitement and fulfilment of the gambler's life requires a number of important "weapons" and tools to give the best chance of success. Amongst these there are a surprising quantity of important superstitions.

Superstition

Never start a new business venture on a Friday, let alone Friday the 13th.

Lore and Sources

We have seen, in the chapter entitled "The Threshold of Belief," how Friday came to be thought of as an unlucky day because of the death of Jesus, and this is also the original source of the superstition that demands that we do not start any new venture on that day. The fact is that most of us would probably wait until Monday simply because it is the first working day of the week, but perhaps our subconscious fears help to confirm this.

Above: *After World War I nations looked back nostalgically to the literal, golden age of monetary stability.* **"We want no change"** *proved the American faith in the reality of gold and the pre-war gold standard. The 1898 Presidential election had been fought over the gold issue, McKinley being backed by business men who favored gold while Bryan the anti-industrial and agrarian candidate chose silver. Underlying the campaign the emotional choice was between male, solar gold and female, lunar silver. Library of Congress.* Above: *Two lucky charms popular in the United States at the turn of the century.*

Superstition

Carry a silver dollar or better still gold coin about with you at all times when involved in financial trading.

Lore and Sources

The origin of the idea that good luck resides in a lucky coin comes from the ancient shipping world in which, almost without exception, a new ship was built with a gold coin at the base of the mast and another within the bedding of the keel. The mast and the keel were the two most vital parts of the ship and therefore required the greatest good fortune. But there was a distinct difference, originally, between gold and silver, in terms of the flavor of their fortune.

The very earliest forms of alchemical belief carried with them the deepest and most profound magical content. Alchemy, explained in its most simple terms, is the changing of base metals such as iron or bronze into gold. The alchemist literally attempted, through the use of chemicals, potions, incantations, and spells, to make this physical transformation. In a more subtle interpretation, it could be seen as any form of transformation including spiritual, physical or psychological, and alchemy is truly at the base of all human change, including our appreciation and understanding of superstition.

Gold was the metal of the sun, solar energy, and light. It therefore symbolized incorruptibility and when formed into a crown or a beautiful necklace, gave dignity, honor, wealth and success. Still today, the wearing of gold in the form of a watch or any other form of jewellry gives the wearer a sense of these qualities. The gold coin, therefore symbolizing incorruptibility and dignity, success and honor, was an ideal item to give the ship the maximum good fortune. It must therefore also help the businessperson to succeed.

Right: *Worship in the cathedral of the Almighty Dollar.* Above: *The oldest 'dollar' in currency. This Maria Theresa silver dollar, minted in Vienna in 1751, still circulates as currency in parts of the Middle East and East Africa.*

Silver, on the other hand, in alchemical terms, represented the passive power in nature and the female principle or the moon. In order for the silver dollar to succeed as a lucky charm, its holder must therefore contain a strong element of calm in business matters, perhaps being someone who has already achieved considerable wealth.

Superstition

American workmen within the steel industry twist their suspender before taking a potentially dangerous climb.

Lore and Sources

This simple act is inherited from the knots tied in handkerchiefs which we remember brought good fortune (or alternatively bad fortune).

sacrifice to the sea gods. For every new ship a young boy would die in this violent fashion. A champagne bottle is a far more joyful version of the original. And the words that are spoken as the bottle crashes down – "I name this ship the SS Enterprise." The name must never be changed or bad luck will ensue.

Names are of fundamental significance within the ship-building and shipping industry, including the names of the officers. One of the most dramatic source references to this superstition was born during an English sea engagement against the French in 1757. The ship was named "The Terrible", the captain's name was Captain Death, while one of the officers was called Devil! As if this was not enough, the ship's surgeon had the melancholy name of Ghost, and finally the ship had been fitted out at "Execution Dock." The disastrous result of this unfortunate ship's poor fate was celebrated in a sea shanty entitled "Captain Death."

Superstition

Breaking a champagne bottle across the bow of a ship as it is launched brings good fortune to the ship and all that sail in it, provided that the name is not changed.

Lore and Sources

Champagne is considered a lucky wine. The bottle, the cork and the wine itself all have fortunate connotations and are therefore chosen to celebrate almost any special event or ritual, including childbirth, baptism, and marriage. The significance of the ritual of launching a ship with a bottle of champagne lies both in the smashing of the bottle across the bows and the words that are spoken as the act is performed.

The significance of the smashed bottle comes from the ghastly ritual that demanded the death of a boy against the side of the ship as a blood

"His ship was the Terrible, dreadful to see,

His crew were as brave and as gallant as he.

Two hundred and more were their good complement

And no braver fellows to sea ever went.

Each man as determined to spend his last breath

In fighting for Britain and brave Captain Death."

Opposite: *A typical scene from the great days of sailing painted by Samuel Walter in 1835, Maritime Museum, London. Many of the old sailing traditions which were peculiar to sail have somehow come down to us today – even to the word sail-or. It is still considered to be lucky to touch a sailor, especially for a girl – a custom rigorously upheld by seamen.*

Above: **In Peril** *by A. Grimshaw, 1879, Leeds City Art Gallery. A scene, only too familiar on any coast in the days of sail. Even today Scottish sailors share the belief that whistling can summon the wind or even a storm. In Caithness no wife would dare to blow on cakes when baking for fear her husband's ship might get caught in a hurricane.*

State-Side Lore

HERE ARE SOME SUPERSTITIONS that have survived to a greater extent in the United States than in other parts of the world, together with a few which have been altered through their trip across the Atlantic.

Superstition

Cut the hair of the dog that bit you.

We have seen, earlier in the book, how hair can work as an important superstitious substance, but in this case, the story is less about the hair than the bite.

Lore and Sources

Superstitious lore loves the concept of "like cures like". Put another way, we believe that if something bad happens to us we will best cure the problem with more of the same. The belief is borne out by the medical principle of innoculation in which carefully measured doses of the offending virus are injected into the body in order to build up resistance against the disease.

The original source of the superstition arises out of a story of a man who was bitten by a dog. He grabbed the animal, cut its hair and used the hair to staunch the flow of blood. He kept the hair thereafter in the belief that it would provide healing qualities for any wound he or anyone else might sustain.

Superstition

Breaking an American mirror may not bring bad luck.

Lore and Sources

Deliberately breaking a mirror in the United States is not a dangerous thing to do, even if the breaking was an accident, and as long as you find a folded five-dollar bill and make the sign of the cross, all will be well. The five-dollar bill, among all the currency, has the greatest good fortune and replaces gold and silver as we saw earlier in this chapter.

Left: *A drawing from the **Book of Nonsense** by Edward Lear. One superstition which has withstood the test of time is that the best remedy for a bad hangover is to have another drink. The efficacy of this remedy is seldom questioned.*

Right: *A woodcut from the Lubeck Bible of 1494 shows **Jacob's Ladder**. By passing under a ladder the intruder breaks the essential and mystical triangle which must bring with it the worst of luck.*

Superstition

The dangers of ladders.

Lore and Sources

Climbing a ladder with an odd number of rungs in some areas in the States is considered very lucky whereas walking beneath one is not. The origin of the ladder superstitions derives from the fear of gallows. In Europe and America during earlier periods of history, the gallows were high enough to require the use of a ladder to place the rope in the correct position, and the dead body, once hung there and presumably rotting after death, would have to be brought down with the aid of a ladder. Anyone walking beneath the ladder might face death in more ways than one, thus the remaining superstition.

Superstition

That the body will be made healthy by the use of filters, potions and magic.

Lore and Sources

Health and body in America is a cult of its own with a large number of beliefs attached to food and physique that clearly arise from our most primitive medical past. "Growing pains" are still held to be a real factor within the trials and tribulations of the young, while many still believe that to tie a piece of red string about any part of the suffering body will relieve pain, and that cotton will deal with rheumatic troubles. We have seen the sources of tying thread about parts of the body earlier in the book as inherited from the spinning of thread.

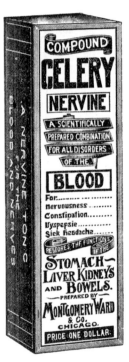

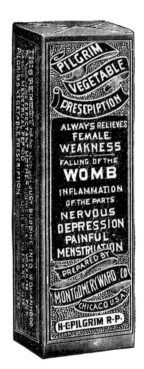

Aphrodisiacs range all the way from avocados to garlic and even include substances which at best will produce the most awful stomach aches.

Various favorite remedies, lotions, linctus and prescriptions of the 19th-century. The rose has always signified purity so the advertiser of 1892 played upon that particular superstition in order to sell his product. The pills actually only contained aloes, soap and powdered ginger, costing a mere twelfth of their sale price but their success went far beyond the ingredients. They often worked because the patient believed they would work.

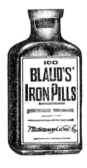

ALL IN A DAY'S WORK

IN THE PAST FEW YEARS both the United States and Europe have suffered from the problems of recession, "tightening our belts" to deal with the threats of bankruptcy, expensive loans, and learning "to make ends meet." Such conditions tend to emphasize the necessity to observe superstitious belief more carefully, for every chance must be taken to win where losses are the rule.

Superstition

Placing shoes on the table is bad luck.

Lore and Sources

Be especially careful, as we learned in the Introduction, not to place shoes on the table before going to work, for this will bring a bad day, and you may even lose your job as a result. The origin of this superstition was the habit of placing the shoes of the deceased on the coffin.

Superstition

Important precautions for store owners.

If you are a shop owner don't sweep the sidewalk until the end of the day, or you may sweep away the day's trade. As a tailor or clothes manufacturer you must work on the left side of the garment before the right, and never twist a hanger around and around by the metal hook or you will wind up the company.

Never whistle at work or you may whistle away the work, and watch out for accident-prone people for they may jinx the office or factory with their presence.

Lore and Sources

All these avoidances and doubts derive from the same idea, that to do or not to do certain things is a way in which we, the vulnerable humans, may exact a certain influence over fate, that unpredictable presence in life. Jinxes can apply both to people and things, such as particular machines that always seem to go wrong and cause accidents, so that in a way we have managed, in modern life, to maintain similar ideas to those that existed thousands of years ago. Fear is the essence when we endow an inanimate object with forces beyond its capacity and give a simple piece of metal or wood almost human characteristics. Originally we gave such powers to trees, rivers, and even rocks, granting each of them spirits and gods to protect us against their unpredictable behavior.

Left: **The Red Model** *1937 by Rene Magritte, Brighton Art Gallery, England.* Below: **Office at Night** *by Edward Hopper, Walker Art Center, Minneapolis.*

Superstition in the workplace is in fact an important aspect of how efficient we are. Time and motion studies of corporate efficiency programs would benefit greatly from a broader understanding of how the average individual sets up his or her day according to almost silent belief systems, belief systems which are nevertheless common to most of us.

The riskier the profession, of course, the higher the level of superstitious observance. Window cleaners have a complete code of behavior which relates to the dangers inherent to scaling tall buildings:

1. If you feel that there is going to be some danger during the day, don't climb ladders.

2. Avoid any area where another window cleaner has had a fall.

3. Always erect your window-cleaning equipment in exactly the same way, for changing the routine brings bad fortune.

It's clear that the above three rules have a strong basis in superstition, but they also have an important practical element as do many workplace superstitions that going to work with a bad feeling may produce foolish mistakes. Places where previous window cleaners have fallen may be dangerous places, and altering the mechanical routine for erecting a cradle or ladder may cause the implement to be erected badly and therefore dangerously.

The construction profession still sometimes puts garlands of flowers on the top of newly erected buildings in order to offset bad luck and keep away evil spirits from the new occupants. Earlier versions of this were much less pleasant, as in Roman times new buildings were often set up with the foundation endowed with the body of a young child set into the ground. Going back still further the tradition is probably connected to the earth rites performed by Iron Age people which were performed as they collected Mother Earth's diurnal metals from the deepest mines.

As we have mentioned, whole rituals had to be undertaken to ask permission for the metals and

ores to be "stolen" from the bowels of the planet. We might even add that to erect any building or make any construction upon or beneath the surface of the planet is to invite the gods or Earth herself to object and destroy the construction. In the 1950s in England a movie was made to commemorate this tradition when the London subway system was becoming more and more established as a form of public transport. "Quatermass and The Pit," a movie first shown in the 1950s, had as its plot the discovery of an alien space ship buried inside one of the subway stations and the finding that the occupants of the craft had been preserved after hundreds of years, only to rise into the sky amidst local chaos and destruction in the form of horned devils. Who says we are no longer superstitious? And of course, the most celebrated of all building superstitions must be the story of the building of the Tower of Babel, too tall to be allowed by God to continue upwards toward heaven itself. Mankind must stay on the earth, suffering and troubled and as far away from paradise as possible.

Left: *15th c,* **Illumination from the
Bedford Book of Hours**.
Above: **Tower of Babel** *1563 by
Pieter Breughel.*

Superstition

Dangers in the theater.

The arts professions are probably the most advanced in matters of superstition, especially actors and actresses. Within the holy temples of the theater there is barely a moment when doubt and fear do not hang about the heads of the players. Never say "good luck" before, during or after a performance, and never, ever refer to the play *Macbeth* by name but always call it "The Scottish Play", for fear of death.

Lore and Sources

Offering good luck is for sure going to attract the attention of the gods who will want to have fun with one of their favorite earthly arts, by denying that good luck to its players.

Another version of the above can be applied to the writing profession where authors are rarely willing to discuss the content of the book they are engaged in writing for fear that it will either be copied or that speaking of it will once again attract opposing forces.

Superstition

The dangers of photography.

Lore and Sources

Photographers will still refuse to take pictures of a woman in her wedding outfit before she married because of the danger of tempting fate by anticipation. This is sourced from the primitive concept that to take a picture of any kind is to steal the soul from the subject.

Opposite: **Frontispiece to The Wits**, attributed to Francis Kirkman 1662. Above left: **Macbeth** meeting with the three witches who foretold his doom. Above: Belgian poster for the 1979 production of Macbeth. Far left: **Ellen Terry** as Lady Macbeth in 1888 and **Sarah Siddon** in 1812.

FOR WHOM THE BELL TOLLS

LOOKING AT SUPERSTITIONS related to travel we must orient ourselves somewhat to the change in circumstances between when the beliefs originated and the modern world, for the differences are great. Today, we think in terms of "living in medieval Europe". Europe or the United States are acceptable concepts to us, but for those who actually made their lives during the early part of this millennium, there was no United States. There was barely a "Country" so far as common awareness was concerned. For those living within two or three miles of a city or town, there might be a conscious awareness of it, but otherwise an entire life would probably be spent without travelling more than a short distance from home.

Travel was to and from the local market – whatever ground could be covered on foot (known then as "Shanks's Pony") or at best aboard a pony or donkey with a cart attached behind. The nature of the fears and rituals were confined to a generally narrow span of existence. So it is out of this that our modern superstitions surrounding travel have grown.

Accidents happen in threes, vehicles should be well named, one that has been in an accident should be burned by the roadside, and so on. But as time went on the modes of transport grew larger and able to cover longer distances, and yet the beliefs surrounding them remained the same.

Bells to the fisherman are probably the most evocative of instruments, for they toll for death, and many a gruesome story has been penned that tells a sailor's end at the hands of a ghostly gong beneath the waves. And yet these bells began everlasting life within the church, where they would chime at funerals.

Any ship that has suffered accident or death aboard under conditions that leave a bad feeling will have problems in the future, both from a lack of sailors and passengers, and should by ancient rites be burned and never sail again.

And in the same way ancient traditions still surround travel by sea, an even greater degree of faithful irrationality continues to surround the most modern form of travel yet, air. Falling into the sea is one thing, but falling out of an airplane is another!

All the systems that work for a ship also work for the airplane, such as breaking a champagne bottle across the hull and then "rolling out" the craft before its first flight. Flight attendants never say emotive words like crash or accident before going on a flight, and dreams of any kind of accident should never be related before a flight. Taking flowers on board a plane is discouraged, especially bunches of red and white colored flowers.

One of the most popular amulets in existence is the St. Christopher medallion, and aboard the average jumbo or Concorde, with its astonishing technology and its computerised wizardry with every possible safety factor in place, one item that you will often find about the person of many passengers is a magic amulet. What science cannot do, superstition will fulfil.

Right: *Watercolor from a 17th c. miniature showing a litter of the time of James I. Each type of transport has its own set of beliefs but the adoption of whether one drives on the left or the right seems to depend upon geography. The British have doggedly resisted most of the rest of the world by driving on the left even when it is known that the left is unlucky. It does not seem the excuse that 'this leaves the sword arm free' is particularly convincing today.*

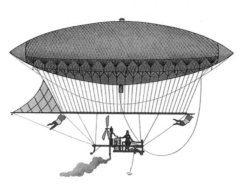

ALL IN THE GAME

BACK IN OLD ROMAN TIMES, when centurians and slaves fought to the death in arenas and poor unfortunate criminals were eaten alive by lions, sport was a tense affair and therefore filled with rites and rituals. As mankind grew more sophisticated and "civilized," so his playfulness relaxed and sports became the pastime of gentlefolk. But once the amateur sportsperson became the professional, the tension returned, and today we are back in old Rome again with sports stars being ritually slaughtered on the football field or in the newspaper columns. Those that cheat by using drugs are fed to the lions more quickly than any criminal of the past. And so we see the superstitions of old return to their place in the anxious hearts of men and women who are supposed to be "playing the game" but in fact are as much at work as anyone who does a nine-to-five in Manhattan or London.

In ball games the players will ritually pass the ball from the oldest to the younger player and bounce it three times and then touch the goal posts for luck before starting a game.

Professional football players tie themselves up, literally, as tight as their bootlaces, to rituals and routines that they must observe, before the outset of a game. As a kind of release from tension a particular individual player from a pro-football team will always, before every game, put his left boot on before his right, tie the laces in a special way, demand to be in a certain position when running out onto the field, and insist that two of his fellow players slap his hand as they position themselves on the field. If any of these are not fulfilled, he will play a terrible game. By all accounts he has never failed to fulfil the routine, so one wonders how he knows about failure.

If we look at the crowd surrounding any kind of field sport such as football or baseball, we can't help but notice the astonishing costumes, banners, flags, chanting, singing, and shouting that accompany the "game." These are incantations to magic, war cries to victory, and spells for success, and they form an integral part of the entirely primitive concept of modern game playing. If the warrior routines were not observed by one team's supporters but were observed by the other, it is entirely certain that the unsupported team would lose the fight, thus confirming Superstition

Rituals and rites are part of the story of game playing in this form. They do create greater energy and the crowd is part of the game, even in the subdued and bizarre Anglo-Saxon religious ceremony the British call cricket where, almost the opposite of football, the supporters must dress in entirely subdued and normal outfits and cannot possibly scream, shout, and chant in the way that football supporters do. Cricket is a much more subtle art and relies for its good fortune on totem-like items such as lucky cricket bats or special caps and leg-pads. Each sport attracts its own character of required superstition.

Opposite: The American painter, Edwin Austen Abbey and his cricket eleven in 1903. Many cricket customs hark back to mediaeval pageantry and the beliefs of chivalry and honor more in keeping with superstitious knights in armour than sportsmen of today. Right: As sports events become more exact and the difference between winner and loser is measured in fractions of a second, so good luck charms are considered just that bit of extra luck to tip the balance. It is instructive to see just how many top athletes do wear small amulets, chains or lucky clothing even today.

But surely there is a natural explanation to all this superstitious release from tension. In the game of golf, the rituals before a player "tees off" might include unwrapping of a new ball, special selection of a particular club that isn't used at any other part of the game, or even watching out for certain signs in nature like a bird song or the rustle of an animal in the bushes. All these signs give the player his relaxation, his centeredness, a kind of meditation that provides a balance in a situation that is demanding and frightening. Just like all superstitions, the chosen and repeated events eventually take over the individual strength of the player, leaving him dependent on them in the same way as the Tower of London is dependent on its ravens.

So, for sports fans everywhere, here are a few of the other best-known anxiety banishers that relate to some chosen games:

Superstitious golf

A professional golfer such as Tony Jacklin will invariably carry some kind of mascot, such as a rabbit's foot or old winning ball. The famous American professional of the 70s, Bert Yancey, wore a copper bracelet which he maintained eased his muscles, but he gave it extra power by calling it his "Voodoo Bracelet"!

The world famous Gary Player actually stated: "Superstition can be a positive force for better golf but you've got to be sure you don't lose confidence by believing your lucky charm has let you down when your game starts to go sour."

When teeing off, the trade name of the ball must be facing upwards and a bad tee off is a bad omen for the rest of the game.

We can see the similarity in this ritual with the aligning of the bed with the floorboards of the bedroom and making sure that the sleeping position is correct according to the magnetic poles.

Numbers also figure high in the superstitious golf stakes, with three, five and seven being favorites for the chosen balls. The number nine is not popular and any high number is considered unlucky for it bodes a high number of strokes in the game.

Never mention the word "shank" or "socket" before a game, for to hit the ball with the club shank or socket is the worst of all golfing habits. We can see that the source of this superstition is the same as that which terrifies actors who are offered good luck. The gods of golf will for sure notice the words and cause the dreaded event to occur.

The artist Kit Williams celebrates the game of cricket in both **Village Cricket**, *1974 and the comic,* **No Ball** *of the same year. These gay reminders of the rural life of England also highlights the point that superstitions remain most powerful in the country. A solitary walk amongst ancient burial mounds over the top of lonely hills at twilight is a very different experience than shopwalking in a well lit New York or London. Ghosts, spectres, fairies and brownies have a hard time to appeal to the imagination of most city dwellers but they appear with the flying saucers in the silence of a lonely moorland.*

Superstitious fishing

Never ask a fisherman how many fish he has so far caught that day and never put the catch-net into the water before the first fish is caught. For float-fishing always use the same faithful float, however battered and broken it may have become. Fly fishermen use familiar flies for the same reason, luck lies in familiarity and past success. And don't use an upside-down bucket to sit on while fishing, or you may turn your luck out onto the ground.

Superstitious darts

Men should avoid playing with women and before a game should always go through a ritual such as adjusting the foot in a particular stance or touching an object away from the game.

Superstitious gambling

Never boast, for failure surely follows. Carry amulets such as silver coins or notes. Never sing during gambling sessions, or you may send your good fortune to another through the air! Never lend another gambler money, or luck goes with it.

The outcome of Gamblers luck is shown in this moralistic Victorian etching by Millais. Two of the legendary "little people" seem to delight in the man's downfall.

THE WHEEL OF FORTUNE

Opposite: **Fishes from the Voyage of the Astrolabe** by Quoy Gainard. Left: *Tarot card showing the **Wheel of Fortune** which has always signified the nature of the gamble. It is not surprising that Fortune is seen as a Lady whom the gambler must woo in order to win.*

Superstitious horse-racing

Never change the name of the horse or offer it good luck before the race, and make sure that any woman associated with the horse (other than the jockey) wears a new dress and carries some form of lucky charm with her when attending the day's race. Jockeys must wear lucky suits, use lucky riding gear, and never put their boots on the floor. Many horse-racing trainers and owners carry a frog's bone around in their pockets, a superstition derived from ancient magic that said powdered frog's bones were a powerful force to subdue horses.

Superstitious sailing

Throw a coin into the water during a storm as a form of sacrifice to the sea gods. If the owner of a boat dies, the vessel must be towed out to sea and either sunk or burned in the style of the Vikings. Then scatter the ashes of the deceased over the place where the ship went down.

In some parts of the Americas, the sailor's weather forecasting is done with the aid of a superstitious rhyme:

"Red sky at morning,
Sailors take warning.
Red sky at night,
Sailors delight."

The original of this quite sensible meteorological forecast was in fact from the lips of a shepherd, not a sailor and went:

"Red sky at night,
Sheep herds delight,
Red sky at morning,
Sheep herds warning."

The modern word shepherd was a shortening of the original two words, for there were also cow herds and goat herds.

*19th-century figurehead of **The Spanish Lady**. Figureheads were believed to embody the spirit of a ship and almost all of them were female. Strangely, however, a female on board ship was considered very unlucky indeed.*

TREADING THE BOARDS

THE FEAR AND TREPIDATION, excitement, and passion of acting in the theater and movies has given new life to some of the most advanced superstitions to survive from our distant past. We already looked very briefly at the fear all actors have of the words "good luck" or naming the "Scottish Play," but there are many more available choices for the would-be anxious thespian, without which he or she may never get the part!

Superstition

A perfect rehearsal is a disaster to an actor, who will invariably not speak the last line of the play so that there is no danger of getting everything right on the night before.

Lore and Sources

This tradition lies very close to the most profound of human religious beliefs left over from early paganism and particularly eastern religious understanding. The ancient masters and priests from the Buddhist and Hindu religions stated that mankind is always in a state of "becoming," never "become," So never perfect. To be perfect is to be dead. Thus an actor will also consciously decline any form of congratulation for a good performance as this invites the notice of the gods. If someone should inadvertently offer good luck the actor under the hammer will utter "break a leg" or some other less friendly admonition.

Superstition

Actors will never look at the audience from between the curtains because they may look through the wrong, unlucky side by mistake.

Lore and Sources

Here again we come to the left/right syndrome in which the right side is the lucky side, as with getting out of bed. A peep-hole is invariably provided for the actor, or it may be "curtains" for the play.

Superstition

Further ominous portents.

Lore and Sources

A telegram delivered on the first night is acceptable if it is yellowed and discolored. The more discolored the longer the run will be. Knots are considered bad luck on stage so that knitting during a script is discouraged. Remember the knots in the wedding ceremony, the fishing net, the steel worker's suspenders?

The original witch's dance written into Macbeth has long since been regarded as the most dangerous scene in any play for the vagaries of good and bad fortune. As long as the dance is performed within the play, it is okay because in this way it is acting. But if anyone allowed the dance to take place off stage, the power of the witch's magic would destroy all good luck.

The theater is a kind of alchemical cauldron of potential magic, for not only does it date back to the earliest times but it is supported by some of the most primitive souls in existence, people one could easily compare with the mystical gypsy races of the past, travelling players for whom life is rarely secure and almost invariably dependent on the most powerful gods and fates.

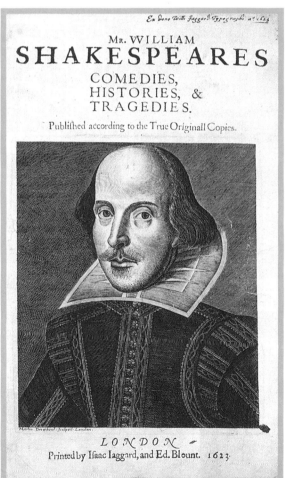

CHAPTER FIVE

RITES OF PASSAGE

The Dance of Life by Edvard
Munch 1889, Nosjonal galleriet, Oslo.
Here we can see the three stages of
women as the maiden, the nymph and
the crone. In the background a phallic
reflection of the female moon suggests
the major rite of passage which is so
much enjoyed by superstitions.

IN THIS THE FINAL CHAPTER of the book we chose the very heart of the matter to occupy our interest. The rites of passage from birth to death are filled with the most primitive of human conditioning. Therefore they contain the most fascinating lore and sources, from birth, youth, marriage, through maturity, old age, and death we face the milestones of life. Every myth and story surrounding these events grew from the birth of mankind itself.

But as with everything that is connected with superstition, we cannot treat it in an organized fashion, at least not from a rational viewpoint. The organization we can chose is that of reality as opposed to science, and the first subject in the reality of the rites of passage is love.

SEASONS OF LOVE

MORE THAN WORK OR PLAY, more than home and country, and often still more than even the body itself, we cherish and desire love.

And of all human activities (if love can be called an activity) we surround love in a greater variety of doubts, insecurities, and superstitions than any other. All the way from the tenderness of courtship to the creation of children and family and the care of friends, we have taken so many ancient lores and pagan rites to our hearts that we make love affairs minefields of catch-points and trip-wires. So pay close attention to the coming chapter, for without this understanding you will never find that one true love.

THE DEVIL LOVE

TO PROVIDE SOME ELEMENT of reassurance to the would-be lover we may start with a few of the connections between love and evil that may help define the perimeters of the human psyche in relation to relationships.

In ancient belief systems the devil or his attendant demons was generally responsible for everything that ever had or would go wrong in life. This state of affairs was brought about by the Christian Church which defined goodness and holiness as something outside the human frame. God was away somewhere over "there" – perhaps in heaven or the sky but in any event a long way from human contact. You either had to be a priest or die before you could find God. So, naturally enough, the opposite of God and good, the devil, was also somewhere else. This neatly diverted responsibility for personal freedom and the source of suffering away from the individual and gave everyone ample opportunity to blame everything other than themselves for whatever took place during life. And we are still doing it today. "I'm unhappy because I can't get what I want," "because you are not the right person for me" etcetera.

But all this is now finished because in 1864 in England the British Privy Council stated clearly in an edict that hell and therefore by implication, the devil, no longer exist! (Unless the devil has left hell and entered the hearts of men.)

"Belief in eternal hell fire was an essential item of Christian belief until pretty recent times. In England it ceased to be an essential item because of a decision of the Privy Council, and from that decision the Archbishop of Canterbury and the Archbishop of York dissented; but in this country our religion is settled by Act of Parliament, and therefore the Privy Council was able to over-ride their Graces, and hell was no longer necessary to a Christian." (Bertrand Russell)

The devil (or rather the Church), however, has had plenty of time to build up a truck-load of doubts in the human mind, so that our fears surrounding the concept of love may still take centuries to relax.

Above left: **Succubi** entering the lascivious dreams of a young virgin. Female devils, spawned by Adam's first wife, Lilith, were supposed to invade the sleep of celibate monks. They stole the semen which the pious ejected in their sleep. In order to prevent these naughty goings on monks and priests would tie a crucifix to their penises in order to thwart the sensual spirits. However it is said that Lilith's filthy laughter rang in many a saintly cloister and priestly chamber as the holy men succumbed in their sleep to what they might suppress in their waking hours. Above: A visiting nightmare and a demon is about to embrace a sleeping woman in this painting by Henri Fuseli. The Goethe museum, Frankfurt-am-Main.

RINGS OF TRUST AND VOWS OF FEAR

Superstition

The wedding ring.

Why do we wear a ring or rings about the finger to signify engagement and marriage? We learned in Chapter Two about the wedding-ring finger being the "medical finger", thereby enjoying the only direct contact with the heart, but why was the ceremony for giving the ring such an important one? What was the original essence of such an exchange?

Lore and Sources

In the twentieth century we have lost most of the deeper significance implied by courtship. Romantic love was once seen not only as a kind of mating ritual which would prepare the couple for the nuptial bed and a lifetime of sexual union, but also as a real and practical preparation for the change from single existence to shared existence. The whole process leading up to the taking of the woman's virginity by the man was so fraught with complex and deeply religious rituals that the placing of the rings on the couples' fingers acted as a kind of final climax prior to the sexual penetration. The man, after all, was depriving both God and the earth of the woman's body, for in early pagan rites and later Christian beliefs those were the only other two places that a woman could go.

The circular rings were exchanged as an outward sign of fidelity but also as a symbolic entrustment between the two; a gift of precious metal under the sight of God.

"A contract of eternal bond of love,
Confirm'd by mutual joinder of your hands,
Attested by the holy close of lips,
Strenghten'd by interchangement of your rings;
And all the ceremony of this compact
Seal'd in my function, by my testimony."
(Shakespeare's Twelfth Night)

Swinburne in his "Treatise of Spousals" suggests that:
"The form of the ring being circular, that is round and without end, importeth thus much, that their mutual love and hearty affection should roundly flow from the one to the other as in a circle, and that continually and forever."

The problem today, however, is the concept of "forever" in relationships. When marriage was bounded by God and harassed by the devil, couples remained in bondage, the rings firmly about their spiritual contracts for fear of hell or high water. Outside the marriage there was failure, scandal and rebuke, and the Church would surely never marry you again to someone else. So you lived, literally, in sin.

There was an Old Person of Tring,
Who embellished his nose with a ring;
He gazed at the moon
Every evening in June
That ecstatic Old Person of Tring.

Left: *From the **Book of Nonsense** by Edward Lear.*
Right: ***The Bridesmaid** by John Everett Millais, Fitzwilliam Museum, Cambridge. Here the bridesmaid is pressing the wedding cake through the ring nine times, which was a superstition common to the unmarried virgins of Victorian England. This act would ensure that the girl would meet her prospective love and would be married within the year.*

Such is Love

Ainsi est l'amour

Superstition

The kiss exchanged between bride and groom after the wedding ceremony.

Lore and Sources

The kiss that is given by the bride to the groom at the end of the wedding ceremony originates from the earliest times when the couple would actually make love for the first time under the eyes of half the village! To be sure that they consummated the marriage by sexual union, several local people had to witness it, or the marriage was not seen within the religious rituals of the time to be finalized. The kiss in church is all that is left not unnaturally in this day and age of greater reserve, for making love in a church or beneath the eyes of the relations might be deemed as slightly excessive. But still, the giving and receiving of rings and the final kiss from the bride is, under modern marriage law, not sufficient. If the couple leave the church or registration office and part company then and there, never

Kissing Lovers *by Dante Gabriel Rossetti. This study is inscribed with the verse:*

Around her, lovers, newly met
'Mid Deathless love's acclaims,
Spoke evermore amongst themselves
Their rapturous new names.

climbing into bed together, the marriage is technically and religiously null and void.

These customs, ring, kiss and passion, date back further than history can suggest. The Romans, Greeks, and Egyptians all used rings. Many belief that Cain, the son of Adam, was the first to use the ring for marriage. If we follow archeological studies of Sumerian lore, this would date the wedding or engagement ring to about 10,000 years ago. That's a pretty old superstition.

Originally the ring was placed first on the thumb and then the forefinger, then the second, and lastly the third where it was to remain. No mention is made of the timing of this change of fingers or reason for it, except that once the medical profession discovered that the third finger didn't have a nerve connecting it directly to the heart there was thereafter no particular reason for employing it in any romantic connection. Once again, science destroys the rose.

Superstition

Throwing confetti over the bride and groom.

Lore and Sources

As much as we still follow the rituals of the marriage ceremony, we also keep up the ritual of throwing confetti over the head of the newly married couple. The original ritual was to throw wheat over the bride only, as a direct symbol of fertility, that she would give forth young in the way that wheat gave forth bread.

Superstition

The significance of the wedding cake.

Lore and Sources

The wedding cake also comes from a similar tradition where the bride was brought "bride-cakes" by guests as symbols of fertile union. The modern wedding cake in all its elaborate splendor is the equivalent.

Left: ***Traditional corn maiden*** *in a wedding dress set within the sacred oak with the mistletoe above.*

Far left: Wedding dress *of the late 19th-century.*

"Two lusty lads, well dressed and strong,

Step'd out to lead the bride along,

And two youngs maids of equal size,

As soon the bridegroom's hand surprise."

(The Collier's Wedding)

Superstition

The presence of bride's and bride groom's attendants.

Lore and Sources

Bridesmaids and the so-called "Best Man" were both born of Anglo-Saxon tradition, though once again the source is quite different and indeed more beautiful than the modern remains.

The bridegroom was brought to the church or ceremony by a brides matron or brides woman who was flanked by an army of bride's-maids. Their task was to see that the groom got to the church on time, and in the same way the bridegroom's men, now known as the best man (there used to be several), was responsible for bringing the bride to the church.

In Sweden during medieval times, weddings took place at night and the "groomsmen" were responsible for providing light from torches that were placed above the altar. These "best-men" were also known as "bride-knights," with the attendant tasks of looking after the woman who would be the bride.

Left: *Bridal wreath from the Englishwoman's Domestic Magazine of 1870.* This page: *Wedding charms. The Centerpiece is titled "Honeymoon."*

Superstition

The preparations for the wedding ceremony and the ceremony itself.

Lore and Sources

The wedding ceremony is one of the most potent rites of passage which carries the man and the woman from one state of existence to another and therefore is surrounded by all the taboos that are associated with such a change. Whenever we pass through such a major life-change, according to ancient lore, so the devil is most present, even if the British Privy Council has decreed he no longer

exists. This can be only a devilish device to hide his existence. The sacred traditions must therefore be observed to the letter so that no mistake is made in any part of the ceremony.

Even before the bride gets to the church she must observe certain rules, such as never allowing herself to be seen in her wedding dress by her prospective husband prior to the ceremony. She must not look upon herself in a mirror once fully dressed for the wedding, for this is the same rite of anticipation that we have seen in other situations whereby she may project the image of herself onto a mirror as a married woman before it is true and the gods may come and challenge her right. The only way she may have a last look at herself is by leaving her gloves or some other item to the side. She may not be perfect for in the eyes of ritual "becoming" is what counts.

The traditional bride today still wears the veil over her face, and not simply from a desire for elegance but because of the most important fear of the evil eye, the devil once more, or simply the jealousy of rival spinsters who once might have been witches. The veil works to protect both the bride from outside evil and to protect the world, her husband to be and her friends and relations from her own psychic influence.

The tradition that states she must have "something old, something new, something borrowed, and something blue" derives from bringing all the available mystical influences into her possession. Something old is the past, something new the future, something borrowed represents the present, and the color blue means purity.

Left: *Victorian Love Token.*
Right: *The Wedding* 1904 by Henri
Rousseau, Musee de l'Orangerie,
Paris.

Above: **Strict Privacy**, *Rue Marcelin Berthelot, Montrouge, 1945 by Robert Doisneau.*

Superstition

Meeting the chimney-sweep brings good luck to the marriage.

Lore and Sources

Once upon a time the bride and groom would arrange for a chimney-sweep to come to the church doors and be available as they left the ceremony, for to meet with one was the best of good fortune. The origin lay within the fact that the sweep was a guardian of the hearth and the fire which were once the very center of domestic magic.

The sweep was supposed ideally to walk a short distance with the bride and should be approaching her when seen, and not walking away from her. He should also be dressed in his sooty clothes and with a blackened face or the ritual was not fulfilled.

The Fertility Chair, *Durham England. Once said to have belonged to the Venerable Bede this oak chair is believed to influence both marriage and fertility. Unmarried girls would place splinters from the chair beneath their pillows in order to dream of their future husbands. Brides sat in it immediately after their wedding to ensure fertility while pregnant women used an infusion made from soaked splinters to ease the pangs of childbirth.*

16th c. **Miniature** *of a courtly ceremony closely resembling a wedding reception of promenading couples.*

Superstition

Requirements of the newly-weds.

Lore and Sources

The newly married couple, once past the ceremony, must continue to observe certain customs. They must send pieces of the wedding cake to absent friends and relatives, for to do so is to include each recipient into the luck of the bride and groom. The bridal bouquet has come to us down the ages through a number of twists and turns. Remember the groomsmen or bridal knights that we spoke of earlier in this chapter? The tradition was once that these men would have to fight for the bride's garter at the end of the ceremony and the winner would achieve great good fortune, but the decorum required by the Christian Church demanded that this was altogether too lusty. Eventually the bride simply threw a flower garland instead of her garter, to the nearest brides maid, who would thus take up the good fortune of the bride.

Superstition

The speech at the reception.

Lore and Sources

Among the comedy movies of the recent past that contain scenes of wedding parties or receptions, there is invariably a speech made by someone in the cast of guests that is filled with ribaldry and bad, often dirty jokes. One might not expect such an act to have much to do with ancient ritual, but in Rome during the latter part of the millennium before Christ, there was always present at a wedding an official joker whose task it was to make rude jokes to the audience in order to divert the interest of the gods from the newly married couple and therefore ensure their safety from evil influences.

Opposite: *June Night* by Henry Koerner, Dallas Museum of Art. Above: *The Lovers* from four separate Tarot decks.

Superstition

The honeymoon.

Lore and Sources

And then comes the honeymoon, of course. Here again we might imagine this to be a modern ritual concerned with vacations away from home and breaks from the routine, but then why call it a honeymoon? Very simply because during the period of one whole moon following a marriage, all the guests, married or otherwise were to drink honey, an aphrodisiac in the northern part of Europe.

And last but not least, each anniversary of the wedding was given a substance to commemorate the years in joy together (hopefully).

The items were intended to be given by each party to one another.

First – *cotton*, second – *paper*, third – *leather*, fifth – *wooden*, seventh – *woollen*, tenth – *tin*, twelfth – *silk or fine linen*, fifteenth – *crystal*, twentieth – *china*, twenty-fifth – *silver*, thirtieth – *pearl*, fortieth – *ruby*, fiftieth – *gold*, seventy-fifth – *diamond*.

Left: *A traditional English honeymoon would be held at the seaside.* Bottom left: *A young married couple wed on the very day that Britain went to war with Hitler.*

This page: *In the past the honeymoon re-established the woman as a sexual being while she had not been allowed to be anything but a virgin before this. These tattoo designs tell the story of the underlying currents of male thought. These saucy creatures with the wicked serpent in close attendance show that in the male mind there is a second wild and sinful aspect of a woman. It is this lustful side which the honeymoon is supposed to reveal.*

EROTIC LORE

IN THE MEDIEVAL FOLKLORE "mind," carefully compounded by the cautions of the Church, marital sexuality was the only sexuality. The bonds of marriage were presumed to lead to nuptials, which in turn brought a consummated coupling and then presumably children.

The passing on of erotic folk-lore was undertaken largely between mother and daughter in a kind of whispered secrecy to satisfy the taboo nature of the subject. During puberty the young girl was surrounded by a mixture of fear of rape and the subsequent loss of her virginity, which would make her unsuitable for marriage, and a gentle romantic courtliness which persuaded her that love occurred in the cherished surroundings of the home.

Old wives' tales were the chalice within which erotic belief flourished, for women understood sexuality while men performed the active and aggressive rites which resulted either in disaster or family. One of the most bizarre aspects of sexual superstition arose from something called "ghost lore." Young women were told about or read ghost stories intended to provide a kind of horror which would keep the individual in a state of trepidation with regard to sex. It was believed that phantoms inhabited the homes of the young and that given the "wrong" kind of behavior, the dreaded spirit would emerge from the wardrobe in the bedroom, stand at the foot of the bed, and then presumably rape the young woman as she lay virginal in her bed.

This potent combination of misinformation and tension has given birth, over the centuries, to a marvellous set of superstitions which remain alive today. The Victorian era in Europe kept the whole thing going by suppressing sexuality and thereby making it even more powerful a force, to be enacted in secret and amidst every possible excitement and complexity.

If the body is cautiously covered, then ignorance of its nature will give rise to all manner of beliefs connected to its sexual potential. In Victorian England even the chair legs were covered by "skirts," and women were forced to discretely disguise every aspect of their natural shape. At the same time sexual activity was covertly performed behind every available facade. Ideas regarding the sexual organs and their potency were related to the size and shape of other, more visible parts of the body. For example, large hands or feet, or even ear lobes, indicated large sexual organs in the male and therefore greater sexual potency. A lot of hair on the body and dark-colored hair, also indicated a "hot" sexual capability, so people from the south of Europe with "Latin" qualities were regarded as somehow animalistic in their passions, or hotter simply because the sun shines more in that part of the world. On the female side, a woman with a large mouth was thought to be blessed with a large vagina.

Right: ***Patience and the Passing of Time*** *by Kit Williams.*
Above: ***Hatstand*** *by Alan Jones.*

From the earliest days masturbation was believed to create various unfavorable growths on the body, such as hair on the palms of the hands, together with heart problems and blindness. This fear was also applied to excessive sexual activity of any kind between couples who were making love out of wedlock. These wild assertions were compounded by the advice that as soon as the wedding had taken place there was an immunity to venereal disease.

Put simply, the young woman was better off in wedlock, and once there she was stuck with it regardless of unfavorable conditions, poor treatment by the patriarchal husband, and very probably the necessity to deal with his fully permitted unfaithful behavior. Given the modern free attitude to sexual behavior and divorce, one might imagine that many of the superstitions would disappear, but this is by no means the case.

It is still believed today in several parts of the world that jumping up and down vigorously after sexual intercourse will help prevent pregnancy. Another, medically unfounded superstition states that women who wear contact lenses should not take contraceptive pills. The onset of the killer disease AIDS has no doubt brought back many of the most ancient superstitious beliefs, and for sure the idea of forming permanent and exclusive relationships in order to avoid too much sexual contact with too many people will eventually breed its own forms of fear, all of which will be connected with the primitive past.

Love charms have always been a popular form of superstition among the young. Originally a

girl in search of a lover would place a leaf in her shoe to lure the right man to her. Today the drinking straw is the replacement of the leaf, and a young woman should never knit a sweater or other garment for the man she hopes to marry, for to do so is to once again reflect the anticipated event of marriage and bring the gods to awareness of it.

Far left: *Irish women throw apple-peel into the water at Halloween in the hope that they will form the initials of their future husbands.*
Left: *Pierced hearts, dates, names and suggestible tit bits cover this statue in Paris.*
Above: ***The Cathedral scene from Faust in which Margaret is troubled by Evil Spirits*** *by F.C.Cowper, Private collection.*

THE PRIMARY PASSAGE

AND ONCE THE PLETHORA of provisions against all the sexual taboos has been survived, the happy couple are securely married and the nuptials successfully encountered, we come to the point of it all, the first born child.

During the twentieth century we are still completely subdued by many forms of very unmedical beliefs surrounding birth. We exist in a kind of transitional period where science has not quite found all the answers and therefore leaves plenty of doubt in the minds of the pregnant mother. Can we, for example, will the sex of a child? By wishing forcefully for a girl, we can ensure the birth of a boy. By making love actively a few days before the woman ovulates, we stand a better chance of a female child because the female sperm are sturdier than the male, while if we make love closer to ovulation, the male sperm runs faster and gets there first! No one quite knows whether this is true or false and so the idea lives through doubt.

If a mother wears blue during her pregnancy she will have a boy, and pink will bring a girl. Reading academic studies during pregnancy will help the child to be clever and during this century of renewed psychic belief it is now almost firmly established that a mother enjoys a kind of extrasensory connection with the unborn child, even though there is no way of proving it to be true. It has to be said that perhaps this kind of superstition can certainly do no harm and may actually be part of a greater awareness and concern for the subliminal connections that undoubtedly do exist between living creatures.

Opposite: ***Mother and Child*** *by Mary Cassatt, Musee Nationaux, Paris.* Right: ***Detail from Christening Sunday*** *by James Charles, Manchester City Art Galleries.*

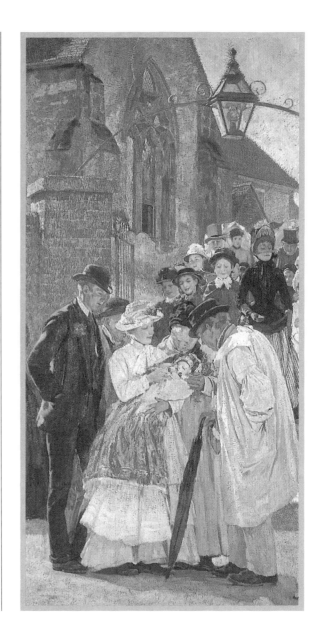

Superstition

It makes a difference at what time or date the child is born.

Astrology has in recent years formed a fascinating part of the upsurge in superstitious belief. The author came across a case of a proposed connection between the stars and birth during the 1970s in which a mother, believing profoundly in the importance of birth signs, refused to allow herself to go into labor until the exact right time according to the horoscope of her unborn child. Lying in the labor – room of the hospital she "held on" to the baby until 6:10 P.M. because up until 6:09 P.M. the baby would have suffered the sun sign of Aries,

Right: *Astrological scene in which the crafts, sciences and occupations associated with each celestial principle is shown.* **Painted table top** *by Martin Schaffner, 1533, Hessisches Museum, Kassel.*

while after 6:10 P.M. he would be a taurus rising sign, and this is what she wanted. It was firmly believed that to give birth one minute later would alter the entire character of the coming infant. Here is superstition in action.

Lore and Sources

Such ideas grow directly out of the oldest beliefs, for originally a child born at the chime of the hours of three, six, nine or twelve o'clock was believed to be blessed with second sight. A Sunday child is gifted with the best of luck whereas one born with teeth already grown will undoubtedly be a murderer.

Victorian photograph of an unknown child, 1870 by a West Country photographer, England.

Superstition

Baptism.

Lore and Sources

We still fervently baptize our young against original sin, without really understanding what original sin is. In the most primitive times the father would undertake the task of carrying the child to the sea and making a sign of the cross in salt water upon the baby's left shoulder, once again providing the infant with some protection against the devil who had already taken up residence behind the poor little child. Baptism, therefore, was to do with direct protection from evil, and was subsequently adopted by the Christian Church.

It was once common practice for baptism to take place almost immediately after the birth. It was held that an unbaptised infant could not go to heaven and if it died its soul would eternally wander the world as an angry spirit. Unfortunately the baptism itself was sometimes the cause of death to infants who were too vulnerable and exposed too soon. At least they were, in such innocence, guaranteed a place above.

Superstition

Naming the child.

Lore and Sources

And given the happy new baby, given the right sex, and provided all sorts of other rituals have been satisfied, we must next find the right name, for this is the first form of identity that will stay throughout the whole life. Many parents spend weeks before the birth and much time thereafter pouring through dictionaries of names, checking with relatives, and trying out all kinds of lavish alternatives before settling on the final choice. The eventual name may have nothing whatever to do with the personality of the child, for this cannot be discovered perhaps until several years into the child's life. Nevertheless we make the name choice according to our conditioned preferences, such as actors or other personalities we admire, relatives that are dear to us, or even names of one of the parents on the basis that "like father like son," possibly one of the most disastrous and superstitious ideas that we could ever have. But in the same way as naming a ship was important, so also is naming a child, for a child that grows up, as many did in ancient Europe, without a name, there is the fear that he or she will somehow never form a character, or worse, be taken away by evil influence to become a stray soul.

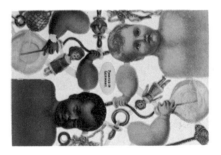

Superstition

Carry the child up the stairs and then down again.

Lore and Sources

New-born babies are still ceremoniously carried up a set of stairs and then down again because of the old belief that a child must go up in the world before it goes down.

Superstition

The rituals for the mother to perform for the protection of her child.

Lore and Sources

Mothers will cut the first locks of a child's hair and stick them into a commemoration book and take the first tooth that comes out and place it beneath the child's pillow to be substituted with a coin by the tooth fairy. These traditions can be sourced from the time when the hair and teeth of a baby were kept throughout the entire life and then placed within the coffin so that the life was completed and the spirit could face Judgment Day having passed through the full cycle of existence.

Superstition

The birthday celebration.

Lore and Sources

We place candles on a child's birthday cake and the child blows them out with a wish. The very concept of the birthday celebration is as ancient a superstition as any, and the blowing out of the candles began with the Greek tradition in honor of the birthday of Artemis, goddess of the moon, marriage, and childbirth, in which special cakes were baked in the shape of the moon and candles were placed on altars within the temples. During the celebration the candles were to be blown out with one breath, and Artemis would then gaze favorably upon her worshippers.

*Below: Kate Greenaway's sentimental illustration of the childhood game "Ring-a-ring o' roses" masks a more sinister reality. The seemingly innocent song is a parody on the awful conditions of the Great Plague of Europe which left, in its wake, a whole collection of superstitions. A ring of rose colored spots was one of the first symptoms of plague. "A pocket full of Posies" reflects the mistaken belief that herbal posies were a protection against the scourge.. "Atish-oo!, Atish-oo!" was the sneezing which confirmed that one was about to die and the last line "We all fall down" was quite literally that we all fall down DEAD! Many such superficially innocent customs and folklore hide equally dark origins. However, the cake and candle in the painting opposite of **Baby's Birthday** by F.D.Hardy seem to have nothing sinister in their backgrounds. Wolverhampton Art Gallery and Museum.*

Left: ***First Steps*** *by G.Neale, Walker Art Gallery, Liverpool. Right: detail from a 17th-century painting of the* ***Cholmondeley Sisters****, Tate Gallery, London. Below: Avoiding stepping on the unlucky gaps between paving stones.*

Superstition

Concerning the colorful toys on strollers.

Lore and Sources

We place our newborn child within specially prepared strollers with all kinds of colorful and noisy devices hanging above the child's face, ostensibly to entertain. But the original idea was to place bells close to the child's head because they would frighten away evil spirits and provide magic charms for protection.

And so it goes on, throughout the life and passage from birth, to early childhood, to the teenage and adolescent years, and into the first relationships which result perhaps in marriage.

Every step of the way we can find enough superstitious beliefs to fill five volumes. Never wear a cardigan inside-out or, if you do, turn in a circle three times before reversing the mistake. In order to give good or bad fortune to another child, stare forcefully at the back of the child's neck. Never walk on the cracks in the sidewalk or the bears will jump up and eat you. Dreaming of teeth means death in the family. If someone knocks only once on the door, never answer until the second knock comes, because vampires only knock once and must not be invited into the house. And as we know, the postman always rings twice!

And then, eventually and inevitably, despite every protection we may draw to our uncertain lives, there comes the final passage.

THE SENSING OF DEATH

THERE ARE SO MANY BELIEFS and traditions surrounding death that it is hard to know where to start. Much of the active manifestation of the fear of death occurred naturally through the two opposing forces within religion, good on the one side and evil on the other. We can hold the Greeks largely responsible for this dichotomy of understanding, for in other civilizations prior to their times good and evil existed as one completeness. In parts of Eastern belief there is still today not the same appreciation of bad and good but a simple acceptance that one cannot exist without the other.

However, in the Western mind darkness and light were forever at war and therefore busily creating tension and fear in all its fascinating forms. The entire vampiric legend has grown out of the shadow of death and its extraordinary fantasies, such as the belief that before death arrives there will be a shadow to warn us, and after death has passed that same shadow may return in the form of a wandering spirit which is capable of reinhabiting the body to produce the walking undead.

There have been literally thousands of stories attested to and witnessed by any number of accounts of the sight of ghosts and especially wrathes of the dead. There are even photographs of ghosts that have stood up to scientific tests, all of which lend authenticity to our most prevalent fears, that somehow death brings something more after life.

The dark angel of death, or the "grim reaper," brings many different manifestations in popular culture such as the dreaded shudder which indicates that someone is walking over our grave, presumably a grave existing somewhere in a time warp that we will one day visit. The modern examination of death has been given a tremendous boost by the numerous accounts of people who have

Opposite top: *The soul being more tempted by what the devils have to offer than the angel in this 19th-century moralistic engraving.*
Below: ***Fading Away*** *by the photographer H.P.Robinson 1858*

somehow managed to die and then return, though whether dying can actually happen and then life once more follow is still highly doubtful. It nevertheless does a lot to our superstitious beliefs. The factor that brings the rituals and rites surrounding death into the most fascinating light, however, is the concept that it is not an ending but a beginning, and the final passage from life is yet only another, rather than the last.

In ancient Egypt, pagan Europe, and old America, the rituals that surrounded burial make it perfectly clear that mankind understood there to be a journey which was undertaken after the living human was "passed away." We still use this same term to describe the dead today, and the way in which burial chambers and graves were stocked with food, tools, and various other items indicates that the original concept of a continued existence of some kind was the most powerful of forces to create lore, a lore that we still give the greatest attention to.

Superstition

Laying flowers on the grave.

Lore and Sources

Flowers are laid upon the grave today as a token of affection, but the original purpose was to provide something living in order to give happiness, and a circular wreath placed upon the front door or laid upon the grave would enclose the spirit against its return.

Superstition

Wearing black clothes or a black band in mourning.

Lore and Sources

It may be that the black band worn about the arm of mourners performs the same function as the wreath of flowers, though it is also a simple convenience to replace the original black clothes that were worn (and still are in many parts of the world) in some parts of Europe for years after a death. The original belief was that the widow of the dead man (men generally died sooner than women) should remain wearing black for up to seven years and remain always at a safe distance of several miles from the grave so that the dead husband's spirit would not wander back to her and pester her, or make her into a vampire. The wearing of black clothes made her less visible to the departed husband.

Superstition

Looking after the dead.

Lore and Sources

The soul passes into a new existence which we living, of course, know nothing about, all the more reason to imagine and fantasize over. Right from the moment of death, therefore, the body must be cared for, for example by never leaving it alone in the house. Someone living should always be present to make sure that evil spirits do not interfere with the dead, and the windows must be left open to ease the departing spirit, the curtains drawn and mirrors covered. The living in the presence of the dead should retain the right frame of mind to create the correct aura out of love for the departing dead.

Right: Sir Thomas Aston's beautiful wife died in childbirth in 1635. She is shown at the foot of her own deathbed while her remaining child, Thomas, holds a navigation cross with his father. The inscription beneath a skull which rests on a black- draped wicker cot reads "He who sows hope in the flesh reaps bones". This hauntingly evocative painting is in the City Galleries, Manchester, England. Above: It was the custom in the 19th-century, in both Europe and the New World, for a white-sashed bearer to walk in front of a child's coffin bearing a white standard. This practice is still observed in some rural areas of England to this day. Black has been the color of mourning for over 2000 years. It was first associated with the underworld but later somber clothes and dark widow's veils were used to prevent recognition by possible angry ghosts.

FINAL RITES

OF ALL DEATH SUPERSTITIONS, the funeral is perhaps the most profound. Here again, we must remember that the relationship between the living and the dead, where death has recently occurred, is that those remaining have a definable responsibility to make sure that the spirit actually manages to depart this life and move onto the next. Nobody wants the soul to become an earth-bound and wandering spirit. Ghosts are traditionally not happy.

The lore, as always, contains a clear practical purpose. If a ghost is "stuck" on earth it will make the life of the living miserable in every way possible. The three levels of requirement, physical, psychological and spiritual, must be fulfilled with every care through ritual, or the ghost in the form of human conscience, plus a high degree of imagination, will make life hell.

The following are a few of the many ideas that surround this complex and sometimes highly romantic belief structure, perhaps giving a small sample of how superstitious we still are in matters of the dead.

Superstition

Moving the dead must be performed according to strict rules.

19th-century design for a Masonic tracing board. The doorway to the mysteries is guarded by a death's head. Opposite: John Dee and Edward Kelly supposedly tried to raise the dead in this engraving from The Astrologer of the 19th-Century.

Lore and Sources

Once buried, human remains were never supposed to be moved to other locations unless a proper ceremony was undertaken, or there was the risk that somehow the soul would need to return or would be disturbed in its eternal rest. One of the best stories surrounding the idea of moving the dead is related in connection with the body of Nostradamus, who was moved by the city father of Salon, where he was originally buried in a church outside the town. The administrators opened the coffin one hundred and fifty years after his death in the year 1700 and found to their dismay a medallion about his neck with the date 1700 imprinted on it.

Superstition

Unconsecrated ground should only be used to bury certain categories of the dead.

Lore and Sources

Those that have been buried within unconsecrated ground will for sure suffer the consequences, their journey to the afterlife being directed down into hell. Traditionally murderers were so buried, and there are many ghost stories, such as the famous movie "Poltergeist," that involve the problems of graveyards that are covered by modern developments without the ground being properly blessed, or the graves moved to other proper locations.

Superstition

Suicide insults the fates.

Lore and Sources

The act of suicide is still today regarded as damaging to the soul as the life has been cut off suddenly and unnaturally so that somehow the fates are insulted. In India, the Hindu faith determines that an individual that has died by his or her own hand will have heavy karma to deal with for many lifetimes before the balance can be redressed. Suicide in India is rare! In many parts of Europe suicide and attempted suicide are still technically crimes,

Ophelia by John Everett Millais 1852. The Pre-Raphaelite image of the final drowning of the mad Ophelia. It is believed that the spirit can leave the body in the company of the Angel of Death more easily in the open air. Often a window is left open for the deceased to leave. One superstition has it that when a funeral leaves a house no one must shut the front door until it returns. If not, then the door will be shortly reopened for another corpse.

and originally therefore the body of the someone taking his or her own life would have been buried in unconsecrated ground, thus insuring a trip to hell – the Western version of bad karma.

Superstition

Ghosts remain on earth because they are in Love with the Living.

Lore and Sources

It is frequently believed that if a mother dies in childbirth, she will remain behind in spirit form to make sure that her child is safe. The same can be said of lovers who die unrequited. Once again, the cinema has represented such an idea in popular form for many years, particularly in the last decade with movies such as "Ghost." The belief has been around since Egyptian times and in parts of pagan

The Lady of Shalott. A photographic composition by H.P.Robinson illustrating Tennyson's lyrical poem of that name. The image created only eight years after Ophelia owes much to Millais in both content and style. It appears that, to the Victorian mind, suicide was an essentially feminine pursuit which might reflect upon the nature of womans' lot one hundred and fifty years ago.

Europe if a mother died in childbirth and the child survived, the poor unfortunate baby would be buried with the mother to make sure that she did not return in search of her child.

SPEAKING OF THE DEAD

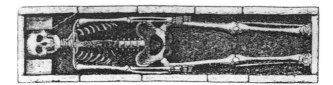

ONCE DEATH HAS OCCURRED then, the living are left with what remains – the corpse. This strange, enigmatic, and disturbing item of life is also subject to numerous requirements in the ancient lore and sources of superstition.

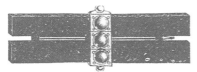

Superstition

How to remove the dead.

Lore and Sources

The corpse, when removed from the death bed, whether it be at home or from the hospital, must be carried out feet first. The human being comes into life head first and must therefore leave the other way. Conversely, people being operated on in hospitals are still today taken into and removed from the theater head first. Corpses aboard ships are considered very unlucky and must therefore be buried at sea as quickly as possible, again, dropping into the sea feet first, or they will bring either bad weather or bad fortune. Many a disaster at sea has been confirmed by the previous death of a member of the crew.

Superstition

Washing the threshold.

Lore and Sources

Women in the rural districts of England still wash the front door step after the body has been removed for burial, thus completing the story that perhaps began with carrying over the threshold.

Superstition

Close the eyes of the dead and never speak ill of them.

Lore and Sources

The eyes of the dead are always closed, for if they remain open after death, then the corpse is said to be waiting for the next life or searching for the next person to die. And never speak ill of the dead but always utter phrases such as "poor man" or "honest man" or "rest his soul" otherwise the soul may come visiting.

Above: ***Three figures*** *from the tomb of a Burgundian Official. Preoccupation with death was intensified after the shock of the Black death in 15th-century Europe.*
Opposite: ***The Dance of Death***, *France 16th-century.*

Superstition

Dancing for the dead.

Lore and Sources

The Romans had some unusual and enlightening ideas about how to make sure that the dead went happily on their way. Instead of looking unhappy and mournful after a death had occurred, they would dance together and sing during several hours in order to make sure that the attendant spirits were fooled into thinking there had been no death at all. This ensured that the departing spirit would not attempt to re-enter the body because so much fun was happening around the corpse. Equally, crying over the dead was a bad idea for two reasons. The sadness involved in tears makes the departing soul unhappy, and the life that exists in the falling tear may cause the spirit not to leave the body. Equally, each relative or friend should touch the dead body to make sure that the final contact dispels all dreams of the dead.

Superstition

Wrapping the body in linen.

Lore and Sources

And among perhaps the holiest of all relics is the linen that wraps the corpse ready for burial, in particular the body of Jesus. The Turin Shroud has formed its own tradition for almost two thousand years, appearing and disappearing in and out of the hands of the Catholic Church and its examining scientists in a, so far, vain attempt to prove the very basis for the belief of Catholicism.

Elaine by J. Grimshaw, 1877, Private Collection. Elaine and Sir Lancelot was a poem by Tennyson in which the heroine dies of unrequited love for Lancelot, who is, of course, in love with King Arthur's wife, Guinevere. Elaine is seen here floating down to Camelot in her funeral barge.

LAST WORD

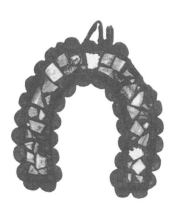

For those who knew of their own superstitious natures, this book has no doubt confirmed them, and for those who denied any knowledge of superstition, it should now be obvious that the rituals, lore and sources lie written between every line of life, and apply to almost every aspect of our day-to-day affairs, very often without us being conscious of it. For superstition is like a beautifully designed petticoat to magical fashion, the hem of the supernatural.

Apart from the obvious magical connections of many of the superstitions we have seen in the chapters of this book, we have also found many practical devices such as medical cures and provisions for a secure way of life in the home. In fact, superstition has a deep connection with human security, for the most substantial aspect of its source is the whole process of man's search for food and the preservation of the body. The festivals and rituals that were employed by pagan man to celebrate and encourage the harvests were the very deepest sediment laid down, so to speak, on the rock of human foundation. Thus their enduring nature.

This is, of course, not intended to suggest that we should be looking over our shoulders at every minute of every day in fear of demons and devils, flying broomsticks or passing magpies, but with an element of intelligence and selectivity, there is a great deal to learn from the ancient lore and sources, for they were originally intended simply as sensible reminders of mankind's place in his world, and contained secret and sometimes partially hidden suggestions of how best to integrate himself with everything that surrounds him.

So whether we believe ourselves to be superstitious or not, in truth, we are bound up within a profound web of ancient lore that operates within our subconscious minds, probably memorized within the oldest storage systems of the brain. These memories are the memories of our most distant ancestors and the world which they inhabited, commanded and feared. With this in mind, we might acquire a good deal of respect for the superstitions, their ancient lore and sources, and this might, in turn, provide us with a more magical and profound vision of the world we live in.

Good luck to you all.

SUGGESTED READING LIST

M.F.K. Fisher, *A Cordiall Water, A Garland of Odd and Old Receipts to Assuage the Ills of Man and Beast*, Chatto & Windus, The Hogarth Press, London, 1983.

A Dictionary of Superstitions, Edited by Iona Opie and Moira Tatem, Oxford University Press, Oxford, 1989.

Philip Ward, *A Dictionary of Common Fallacies*, Vol. I, The Oleander Press, Cambridge and New York, 1980.

Sir E.A. Wallis Budge, *Amulets and Superstitions*, Dover Publications Inc., New York, 1978.

Ernest Crawley, *Oath, Curse, and Blessing*, The Thinker's Library, Watts and Co., London, 1934.

Eric Maple, *Old Wives' Tales*, Robert Hale Limited, London, 1981.

Walter Clifford Meller, *Old Times – Relics, Talismans, Forgotten Customs & Beliefs of the Past*, T. Werner Laurie Limited, London.

Keith Thomas, *Religion and the Decline of Magic*, Penguin Books, London, 1990.

T. Sharper Knowlson, *The Origins of Popular Superstitions and Customs*, T. Werner Laurie, London, 1910.

Douglas Hill and Pat Williams, *The Supernatural, An Illustrated Survey of Witches, Werewolves, Ghosts and Spirits*, Bloomsbury Books, Godfrey Cave Associates Limited, London, 1989.

Eric Maple, *Superstition and the Superstitious*, W.H. Allen, London and New York, 1971.

Felix E. Planner, *Superstition*, Cassell, London, 1980.

Gustav Jahoda, *The Psychology of Superstition*, Allen Lane The Penguin Press, London, 1969.

Isha Mellor, *Touch Wood*, W.H. Allen, London, 1980.

ACKNOWLEDGEMENTS

The publishers would like to thank the following contributors to the book. Whilst every effort has been made to trace all present copyright holders of this material, whether companies or individuals, any unintentional omission is hereby apologized for in advance, and we should of course be pleased to correct any errors in acknowledgements in any future edition of this book.

Photographs: Premgit: 10/1, 12, 13/4, 15, 23, 53, 54, 55, 58, 62/3, 84/5, 92, 104/5, 107, 108, 109, 126, 128, 143, 156, 184, 214, 253. Malcolm Godwin: 202. Science Photo Library: 44. Popperfoto: 49. Syndication International BTA/ETB/SI: 147. Art Directors Library: 174/5, 178

Paintings and illustrations from: The Bodlean Library, Oxford – Bayerische Staatsbibliothek, Munich – Rockefeller Folk Art Center, Williamsburg – Samuel Rosenburg – Philadelphia Museum of Art – Victoria and Albert Museum, London – Illustrated London News Library – Prado, Madrid – Birmingham Museum and Art Gallery – Marquis of Salisbury – De Morgan Foundation – Tate Gallery, London – Gulbenkian Foundation – Museum Boymans-van-Bevningen – Leeds Art Gallery – Bragaline Collection, U.S.A.– Metropolitan Museum of Art, New York – Natural History Museum, London – Blackwood Hall, Melbourne – University of London – Mr. and Mrs Jacob Kaplan – Library of Congress – Nosjonal Galleriet, Oslo – Fitzwilliam Museum, Cambridge – Musee de l'Orangerie, Paris – Dallas Museum of Art – Hessisches Museum, Kassel – Wolverhampton Art Gallery – Walker Art Gallery, Liverpool – Manchester City Art Gallery.